DINGERS
CONTEMPORARY BASEBALL WRITING
THE MOOSEHEAD ANTHOLOGY XI

EDITED BY DAVID MCGIMPSEY

DINGERS
CONTEMPORARY BASEBALL WRITING
THE MOOSEHEAD ANTHOLOGY XI

LIVRES
DC
BOOKS

Cover illustration by Steve Adams. Book designed
and typeset in Adobe Garamond Pro and Myriad Pro
by Primeau & Barey, Montreal.

Copyright © The Authors, 2007.
Legal Deposit, *Bibliothèque et Archives nationales du Québec*
and the National Library of Canada, 4th trimester, 2007.

Library and Archives Canada Cataloguing in Publication
Dingers : contemporary baseball writing/edited by David McGimpsey.
(Moosehead anthology; XI)
ISBN 978-1-897190-15-9
1. Baseball–Fiction. 2. Baseball–Poetry. 3. Baseball–Literary collections.
4. Short stories, Canadian (English) 5. Canadian fiction (English)–21st century.
6. Canadian poetry (English)–21st century.
1. McGimpsey, David, 1962- 11. Series: Moosehead anthology (Montreal); XI.
PS8287.B38D46 2007C813'.0108357 C2007-906658-5

For our publishing activities, DC Books gratefully acknowledges the financial
support of the Canada Council for the Arts, of SODEC, and of the Government
of Canada through the Book Publishing Industry Development Program (BPIDP).

Canada Council **Conseil des Arts**
for the Arts **du Canada**

*Société
de développement
des entreprises
culturelles*
Québec

Printed and bound in Canada by Marquis Imprimeur. Interior pages printed
on 100 per cent recycled and FSC certified Silva Enviro 110 white paper.
Distributed by LitDistCo.

DC Books
PO Box 666, Station Saint-Laurent
Montreal, Quebec H4L 4V9
www.dcbooks.ca

Contents

Introduction

When New York Yankees catcher Yogi Berra was informed that Ernest Hemingway was a "great writer," Yogi allegedly replied, "Oh yeah? For what paper?" Yogi may have not been fully apprised that Hem used Joe DiMaggio as a motivating conceit in *The Old Man and the Sea,* but at least he instinctively understood any truly great writer might have been on the baseball beat. After all, Hemingway was coming to the Yankees more often than the Yankees were going to Hemingway.

The special attraction between writers and baseball is one that has a long hold on the popular culture of America. Long before steroid scandals and iPhone fantasy leagues, Walt Whitman was writing, "I see great things in the game of baseball"–predicting the game would be a tonic to the people and "repair" their nerves. And while repairing to a plate of nachos and a pennant race game sounds like tonic enough, writers have always found more and more to say about the game, finding within its myths and statistics a perfect mirror for the ideals and corruption of the modern world. Through the years of the sport's unlikely and phenomenal rise, no other athletic pastime (except, perhaps, boxing) has seen so many serious literary treatments of its cherished lore.

From Philip Roth to Marianne Moore, from Bernard Malamud to Robert Coover, from Don DeLillo to Mark Twain, writers have continually returned to create moments around the beloved, uncomplicated formations of a game which started out as a refinement on the British game of rounders. Baseball has since become an enormous, corporate entertainment that sees tens of thousands of people gloriously screaming "You suck!" to athletes being paid a quarter of a billion dollars.

Just what makes baseball itself so attractive for writers is fun to consider. Some look to the characteristics of the game itself and see formal compliment: baseball is not clock-bound and, unlike hockey or football (the most popular sports in Canada and the United States respectively), has a more leisurely pace which is claimed by many to be more conducive to the literary imagination. As George Will (himself a fine baseball writer) sees it, baseball is "too orderly for the episodic mentalities of television babies." It's often said then that in the frequent pauses between actions, baseball finds its way into other narratives, whether it's an analysis of arcane statistics, a louche story about a player in a hotel room or even, as the late, great play-caller Phil Rizzuto did when a game was on the line in the ninth inning, to think upon the difficulty of keeping squirrels out of the backyard.

The "ain't over til it's over" aspect of baseball is frequently imagined as a kind "pastoral retreat" from the clock-demands of urbanity, with the game's manicured fields and cold beers becoming a contemporary emblem of ludic escape. With just a simple ticket, or a click of the remote, one can be transported to a spot where, as poet Baron Wormser puts it "forces do not equivocate." Baseball's dependable lines and statistical symmetries, its fairly drawn contests which do not end in ties, conjure a brief respite from unseen (but certain) jury-rigging and its stadiums become shrines of conceptual purity–"green cathedrals" where all action is quantifiable.

Others see the undeniable connection between baseball and literature simply as the natural material harmony between companionable cultural products. Considering the enormous popularity of baseball over the years, one might well conclude it is more surprising there's not *more* writing about it. As such "baseball literature" has the burden of a perceived conflation of the high and the low. Whatever their imagined formal harmonies, there is a cultural dissonance in the way appreciation has been constructed between sports fans and students of literature. True, visitors to the Emily Dickinson home in Amherst, MA rarely wear foam fingers and, just as true, fans rarely refer to the decision to leave Bill Buckner in the 6th game of the 1986 World Series as "problematic."

In this perceived gap, baseball literature has always had less acceptance than its popularity and pedigree would suggest.

The conception of the "literary" as a social and political ideology explicitly meant to advance and maintain the interests of the elite (not just bow-tie wearing Ivy Leaguers) is a fairly obvious impediment to how anything like "baseball literature" could be taken seriously. This kind of snobbery (rarely in the name of preserving Shakespeare and Mozart and more often in the name of articulating the brilliance of *Six Feet Under*), is uncomplicated enough to not need much analysis of its force. The Yogi Berra story is retold, after all, as a kind of moment where Yogi failed to recognize a person of literary rank, with Yogi charmingly speaking common sense. So, for a long time, the elegance and insight of baseball writing was not something which would eagerly be endorsed in literary-circles, where hostility to working class culture, along with undoubtedly bitter memories of being towel-snapped in gym class, would lead to a routine dismissal of sports as the unserious concern of the less gifted. F. Scott Fitzgerald himself would eventually dismiss the work of Ring Lardner (often cited as the best and most influential baseball writer of them all) as evidence of an author who "moved in the company of a few dozen illiterates playing a boy's game."

Baseball writing, despite the turned noses of literary snoots, has flourished through the years. Receiving a big bump in the late eighties, with very high interest in the actual game and new popular movies about the sport and including a predictable niche for literary products about baseball to be marketed, baseball literature is now a respected genre which is taught and studied in universities and which needs no apology.

One of the best things about baseball is that it's actually not like a church or being stuck in a seminar room. One rarely learns about baseball in a determined effort to study it (though Gatsby does in order to fully

Americanize himself) one learns because it's actually fun and interesting in and of itself. As the Woody Allen character in *Zelig* says, "Baseball doesn't have to mean anything–but it's beautiful to watch."

In an episode of *The Simpsons,* former home run king Mark McGwire asks the residents of Springfield if they want to hear him explain the particulars of a conspiracy or watch him hit some dingers (a slang term for home run). The Springfield crowd naturally begins to chant, "Dingers! Dingers! Dingers!" So, in the same spirit of let's get to the good stuff, in this edition of *The Moosehead Anthology* there are some literary dingers, leaving the explanations to the artists themselves. In this collection, *The Moosehead Anthology* is proud to bring together a selection of the finest contemporary baseball writing of the day, in a variety of genres. From George Bowering's classic twist on the tale of the proverbial pot of gold, to Timothy Morris's wonderful recollection of trying to become one of those great baseball beat writers; from Anastasia Jones's wry sidelong look at the cultural shadow of the game to Dave Bidini's celebration of Warren Cromartie, these, and others in this collection, are examples of the great metaphorical capacities of the game–little of it fit for a Kevin Costner movie.

Much baseball writing, and interest in it, arises out of one of the certainties of being a fan of any game–the disappointment of losing. It strikes me that more than the series-winning home run, more than the perfect game, the work in this anthology is notably attracted to the humanizing effects of trying and losing. Coming out of Montreal, undoubtedly some of this sensibility stems from the bitter feelings about losing the Montreal Expos franchise–something referred to explicitly in several of the pieces in *Dingers*. Naturally, this is where a literary artist would turn, as people generally do not bet on the pre-determined outcomes of poems, stories or plays. In the end, the dingers in this anthology are not "about" baseball–baseball is the vehicle of these pieces which intelligently locates the cultural energy of a certain time and place. If, as author Mordecai Richler puts it, "my devotion to baseball does more than Milton can to justify God's way to man,... but is also an occasional embarrassment to me, I lay some of the blame on my being a Montrealer."

D.M., Montreal 2007

From Fallen Angels

Nap stayed in school two years then just vanished. For months she had no word of him, until one day she got a letter from Birmingham, Alabama, where he was playing semi-pro ball. He said he was sorry, that she'd been a sister and mother to him. He said he loved her. He could hardly write though, and nothing passed through the nearly impenetrable block print. He did come back, and there were stormy scenes between them. Things went back to the way they had been, but as he grew to be the one she needed above all others, carefully shaped by her into the lover and protector she'd always, in fact, been to him, he grew away, consumed by a desire to be a ballplayer, to travel, to leave over and over until the past had been obliterated and there was just an exultation of green grass and blue sky, a moment unhooked from all moments before and since. Marie had started off thinking it was stability he wanted, because more than the world that was what she wanted herself. Now she knew when he looked at her that he was without a history, or a history that contained her. He left a final time, this time for Forida for a tryout, and this time she went with him, to Toronto first, then south and out of winter. Now they were in a barn in Virginia. The owls had found a roost in the hayloft, the scuttling of mice had stopped, and dawn was pearling the eastern sky. Nap lay sleeping like a child. He was still just seventeen.

"... Robert Napoleon Lajoie...."

Laughter. Two or three of them laughed a few seconds then stopped. The tall balding man with the clipboard frowned. It was almost as if he didn't get it himself, though he accented the middle name heavily.

Nap stepped forward, away from the baseline. He looked at the coaches, who all looked surprised at how young he was. He had a pair of scuffed spikes slung over one shoulder, his glove dangling loosely from his left hand.

The man with the clipboard spoke again. "Well, this guy's a sure hall of famer." This time everybody laughed. Nap stepped back quickly. "Luis Menendez...."

A dozen more names. All infielders. Nap had no illusions. At this kind of tryout camp everyone got the quick once-over. Out of seventy or eighty, maybe two, three, got invited to camp. And this was only D ball, the deepest minors. If you hadn't made it by twenty you were out, no prospect. Nap was a month short of his eighteenth birthday. Two years of junior ball in Quebec, fresh from the circus, where his agility and co-ordination kept him in the game. He still couldn't hit a lick, so he'd learned to bunt. He was a good base stealer because he measured and took precisely calculated chances, just like on the trapeze or high-wire. If he didn't learn to hit, he wouldn't go any further... *I lay off the breaking ball, low and away....*

They loped out on to the field, four at a time. At the plate a fat old man in a blue Dodgers windbreaker. He had a bruised and scarred old bat, chipped on the handle. The day was early spring cold with a breeze. The clouds moved quickly towards the rickety centre-field fence, over Nap's shoulder. They made him almost giddy. He flexed the old Cooper glove, which felt good, even though he'd had it five years. He'd gone over it the night before in the hotel, rubbing in neat's-foot oil, massaging the cracked leather. The game might be entering its technological age, but the old tools still did the job, and they still had the power to evoke. The old leather and the oil combined as he kneaded, sending up a rich, rancid odour, as much a part of his picture of childhood as the sawdust and animal dung of the circus. What he hung on to now was as simple as that—the strength of memories, the murmuring voices of childhood, sleeping in the warmth of Maria's smoky breath, or sleeping anywhere there was a blanket or a piece of burlap, often only separated by a curtain from a card game, a meeting of midnight schemers, a couple making love. The world had always breathed close on Nap Lajoie. Some mornings he awoke with an arm flung out of the tent or under the curtain, dirt or sawdust in his clenched hand....

He abruptly stopped daydreaming as he heard the crack of the bat. The shortstop moved easily to his right, backhanded a slow, spinning grounder, and fired it cross-body, getting it to the first baseman on one hop. He had a good arm. Nap would have had to stop, plant his feet, throw, giving the runner an extra step. That was why he wasn't a short-stop, not at this level. Second base can hide a mediocre arm. You could get by on good hands and a good head. Of course, this meant fuck all if you couldn't hit.

The next ball was his. He took a step forward, scooped the ball eas-ily and flipped to first. Automatic. When he was out here everything seemed to go in slow motion, the ball rising to meet his glove, as slow and predictable as a planet.

After half an hour the fat man in the blue windbreaker was out of breath. He motioned them all in. Out of twenty ground balls the short-stop had muffed two and thrown two more away, spectacularly. The third baseman had hands like cement and an arm like a rifle. The first baseman had let a lot get by him. He kept getting his feet tangled on the base. Nap hadn't broken a sweat, missed a ball, thrown one away—despite the poor quality of the field. Someone had recently spread a load of sand and pebbles on the base paths. One bad hop nearly got him in the face, but he'd ducked aside and swiped up with his glove in a com-pletely defensive reaction, getting the ball in the webbing, then spun and thrown from his knees. The first baseman had dropped it, but Nap saw the coaches looking his way. "Nice play," one of them yelled. Nap didn't acknowledge any of this. Better to look serious, even possessed. That was the language of this little geometrical universe. You saved the smart-ass stuff for when you'd made it, when you got your picture on the cover of *Sport* magazine. Until then you acted as if you were a nobody. In D ball you were a nobody who made three thousand a year, two dollars a day for expenses. That's if you were one of the two or three who made it out of the tryout camp, and then survived two, three more cuts. Even that seemed to Nap like heaven.

It was nearly dark when they left the park, after an intrasquad game. Nap had gone one for three, a bunt single, and stolen two bases. He'd made some good plays at second, including an unassisted DP on a shoetop liner he'd picked like a cherry. He knew they were watching him now. One of his outs had been a liner down the right field line that the outfielder had caught as it tailed towards the bleacher seats, sodden and sagging and empty in the growing darkness. They called the game soon after.

"Come by the lobby of the Excelsior at ten a.m.," said the guy with the clipboard, looking at nobody. Nap still hadn't figured out if he was in charge or just a flunkey. "The names'll be posted." They all bled off into the dark, as disconsolate as kids after the game, going home carrying their dreams along with the gloves and bats. Nap found himself with Luis Menendez, the shortstop he'd played with. Thinking of how Menendez had hit and run, he felt a sinking feeling of certainty. He wasn't big enough, fast enough. Didn't hit enough.

"That was a good game you had," he told Menendez, "especially the way you turned that double into a triple when the guy in right looked the wrong way."

Luis smiled, rubbing his slim hands along a bat handle. "Yeah, I was lucky I choose right, or he's gonna have me cold." He spoke with a slight accent, but was obviously pretty fluent.

"You Mexican?"

"No, I am from Caracas, Venezuela."

"There's a lotta good shortstops from there. You speak good English though."

"My mother was a teacher in New York. When my father died we moved back to Venezuela. She taught me English, a lot of other things from books. There's no jobs there, so I came back. Now I am trying to make some money playing ball. Where you from?"

"Toronto... up in Canada," Nap said, thinking of Maria. "That's where we were based. I was born in a circus and travelled round till I was sixteen, then I played ball in a junior league for a while."

"My cousin signed with the White Sox, they got a good organization. He got five thousand American to sign. He's back at home now, broke his hand in a fight. Dumb shit...."

Luis and Nap had got to the end of the little side street beside the field. Distant neon, a blue script and a pink flamingo, pointed the way to the centre of town. It was wet and windy. The kind of night to walk. Some of the players and coaches were hailing a cab back into town, but Luis and Nap kept on walking. The traffic was light and they could hear voices, loud and hollow, on the quiet streets. Nap looked hungrily through the lighted windows into the lives of people he scarcely understood, people with families, scheduled meal times, after dinner recreations around the fireplace. Sometimes, where curtains hadn't yet been pulled to, he could see the blue-grey boxes of light that were replacing the fireplaces. Televisions, burning brightly on different channels. He caught Luis looking too.

"You have TV in Caracas?"

"Oh sure. We got a big one at the hotel. Everyone watches the ball games and dreams of playing in the States. That's why I'm here. They don't look at me back in Venezuela, they got too many shortstops, all young, all trying to be like Aparicio. Getting signed, it's like winning at the numbers. You're a big man, got loads of dough to flash around, you got it made, man."

"What's going to happen if we don't make it? Only two or three at the most, they said."

Luis shivered. "I hope they send me to play in Havana. It's too damn cold up here."

"I'm over a thousand miles south," Nap said with an unbelieving laugh. "It feels like the tropics to me. You don't remember New York?"

"Oh yeah, it was cold. And damp. Then in summer it was hot as hell."

"What are you going to do if you don't make it?"

"Maybe I'll just stay here and get a job. I'm an American citizen, my father he was born in California, out in the desert somewhere. He was a cook in the Air Force."

"You mean and give up ball?"

"Shit, man, I'm twenty-three. I play one year in Mexico. Hit .330 then hurt my leg and miss a whole year. Then the team folds when I get back. My mother is sick so I go home. Two whole years I don't play. This is my last chance, man."

"Your mother still in Venezuela?"

"Yeah. She don't want me playing baseball."

"I never knew my mother. She was with the circus but she died when I was less than a month old. The only one I have is Marie, she's a friend from the circus. A few years older than me. We were going to come here together, but she went back. I don't think she can take being a gypsy any more, she said she was starting to shrivel up and not be anyone. Me, I guess I'm different. Anywhere I am is home.... Hey, there's a bar just down here. Let's go have a drink."

"Okay, but not too many, man. If I don't make it I don't want to have a hangover...."

Dear Youppi

Dear Youppi,

I've been meaning to write you for almost thirty years and tell you how much I hate you. Yes, this is hate mail, but don't worry and call the cops. I'm not going to follow this up with any kind of harassment or attack. Maybe you get letters like this all the time. I'm just being up front so you can rip this up or just stop reading like the coward I think you are.

I've been to many Expos games, and had a lot of great times at the Big O. But seeing your dumb orange ass wobbling around was never great. It always mad me sad and angry. You made me feel sick.

Every time I saw you do that dopey slide on top of the dugout I hoped you would tumble onto the field and hurt yourself. The same goes for every time you motored around the field on that ATV, swerving around like a moron. And one time you actually did wipe out! That made me happy. Unfortunately though, you weren't injured.

Sometimes you had it tough on the job; I've heard the stories. Fans would verbally abuse you and sometimes it almost got physical. One time a fan tried to ignite you with a cigarette lighter. All those people are awesome.

Another thing is you're a dirty slob. I saw you up close a few times, and you're disgusting. Your hair is matted with filth, and you look like you just crapped yourself. Now that you're the mascot of the Habs, you don't have to roll around in dirt so much, but I bet you miss that.

Did you ever watch "The Mary Tyler Moore Show"? In the final episode, everyone gets fired but Ted Baxter. That's kind of like you when The Expos left, except I love Ted Baxter. He was funny, and you're not. If you've actually read this far, don't stop now. It ends with me saying you suck.

Up yours,
Jim

Watson's Rainbow

You have read all kinds of stories about some ball player or maybe a whole team that is mired in a slump so bad that it has to be funny, but then maybe it is too long to be funny, and maybe this player consults a voodoo man or makes a deal with the devil or something, and if there is a happy ending it gets really funny again. But do you know the story of Bunny Watson, left-handed fireball pitcher with the Vancouver Mounties in the AAA Pacific Coast League in 1962?

I have to remind you, maybe, that the 1962 season in Vancouver was kind of funny for other reasons. In the second game of a doubleheader on July 18, manager Jack McKeon, who would win a World Series with the Florida Marlins forty-one years later, stuck a radio receiver into a pocket under the jersey of his ace pitcher George Bamberger. It wasn't that Jack was going to tell Bamberger what to do. Bamberger was the most famous pitcher in the Pacific Coast league, and knew more than anyone in the world what to throw at the starting lineup of the Tacoma Giants. Jack just wanted to see whether he could get away with it.

You could look it up. The radio kit was approved by the Canadian government, and had the call letters XM11495.

The Mounties won the game 8-4, if you are interested in that stuff, but this isn't about Jack and Bamby. It's about the fellow that started the Mounties season as their number four starter—and that was back when teams had a four-man rotation, and the starters didn't come tiptoeing off the mound after a hundred pitches.

The fellow in question was Bunny Watson, and if you are an old fart like me, who hung around Capilano Stadium in 1962, you remember a skinny guy with huge arms, about six-foot three, with shoes so big that when he went into his high kick his right foot put a little shadow in the area around home plate.

Okay, if I start to exaggerate, that means I am turning into one of those old-fashioned baseball writers, call themselves "scribes." You are free to complain any time I start exaggerating for comic effect. But Bunny did have enormous feet.

Bunny had been a bonus baby in 1955, getting $100,000 from the New York Yankees, and sitting on their bench for two years. That was the rule: any high school or college kid who got a big signing bonus had to stay with the major league team for two seasons. It worked for Sandy Koufax and the Dodgers: he was a mature fireballer at age twelve, for goodness' sake. The Twins did okay with Harmon Kellebrew, who started on his Hall of Fame career from day one. But most bonus babies sat on the bench, getting up once in a while to pinch-run, or throw a late inning in a 12-0 game.

Bunny Watson got two stolen bases in four attempts in 1955. In 1956 he got into eleven games, throwing fifteen and a third innings, and going 0-1 with a 6.45 ERA. In those days the legal maximum for a signing bonus was $100,000, but rumor had it that Bunny got pretty near twice that from the Yankees, one of the few teams that could afford it. You can figure out how much he was getting paid per inning. Don't forget to factor in his rookie salary, $5000.

In 1957, as soon as he was legally able to, Casey Stengel sent Bunny down to AA ball, where he could get some innings in. He stayed there for the first half of 1958 and then was promoted to AAA; but in 1959, he joined the legion of unknown players sent by the Yankees to Kansas City in trade for future stars. Bunny went down and played for the Little Rock Travelers, a team that was not known for pummeling the baseball, and then he kept coming up to the Athletics, if that is not a contradiction in terms, then going back down, until the Washington Senators moved to Minneapolis and scooped him up by way of waivers. By that time a lot of the young people he was playing ball with were entirely ignorant of his history as a bonus baby.

In 1961 the Berlin Wall went up, and Bunny Watson spent the season with the brand new Minnesota Twins. They even let him pitch over two hundred innings. He felt as if he were back in Little Rock, as the Minnesota hitters let him down, and he put in a record of 4-18. The Twins told him that he was likely to be in the Pacific Coast League for the start of the 1962 season. It had been nearly seven years since he'd got his bonus. After seven years most of the bonus babies were pretty well broke, but Bunny's dad was one of those new-fangled investment consultants with an office in Boise. By December of 1961 Bunny Watson had about a quarter of a million dollars in real estate and a checking account. But he also had an ERA of 5.25.

Every off-season till then, he had spent his mornings running alongside rural roads, and his afternoons chopping wood and doing pushups. In December 1961 he said to hell with it, he was going to try something else. He thought about going to Berlin to visit the home of his mother's grandparents, but the Twins said no deal—he might get stuck on the wrong side of the Wall. So he went to Ireland. He didn't have any great grandparents in Ireland. He just liked the idea of shamrocks and shillelaghs, all the stuff the popular press and advertising people in New York and Boston liked so much. Heck, he had been born four days after St. Patrick's Day. Close enough. He packed all his green clothes and hopped a DC-8 for Shannon.

For a few days he looked around at the Georgian buildings, and sat down in genuine Irish pubs with genuine Irish Whisky, but this was not the Ireland he had always dreamed of. The Ireland he had always dreamed of featured donkey carts and stone fences and peat hillsides. So he got himself a tweed backpack and a stout stick, and began his rural walking, along lanes and on eskers overlooking brownish water pushing against lichen-covered rocks, all that sort of thing. He carried with him two volumes of Sean O'Casey's plays because he had been lucky enough to catch a production of *The Plough and the Stars* in Chicago one night after a day game against the White Sox. When he bought the books in Dublin the young man who took his money had curled his lip when he pronounced the playwright's name.

A good reason for getting out of Dublin was the chocolate bars. He had never seen such a city for chocolate bars. Everywhere you went you saw people eating chocolate bars. On the street, on the buses. Poor people. Well-to-do-people. Business people. Even in the pubs you saw people standing with a Guinness in one hand and a chocolate bar in the other. Bunny had to get away from all this chocolate-munching. He stuck a dozen apples into his tweed backpack and headed for the treeless country.

One foggy morning he was walking on the Esker Riada alongside the Shannon River near the ruins of Clonmacnoise. On foggy mornings in the centre of Ireland it is usually quiet, save for the odd overflight of Irish Air Corps CM 170s often invisible in the mist. But this quiet morning all Bunny heard was the crunch his front teeth made into an Irish apple. Well, that is all he heard until the angry little voice.

He followed this novelty until he came upon a sight that made him want to (a) laugh out loud or (b) turn tail and skedaddle. No wonder he could not make out what the angry little voice was saying. All Bunny could see was the bottom half of a very little person sticking up into the air, legs gyrating, little seat humping back and forth. The creature's top half was poked into a hole in the ground, and the sound that came out was muffled by the tight squeeze, thin in pitch due to the small size of the person it emerged from, and in a language other than English. Irish, Bunny figured.

He put his tweed backpack down on the boggy ground, seized the little ankles, and yanked the expostulating wee fellow out of the hole.

"*Buíochas le Dia!*"

The critter was bashing himself around the head and neck, trying to get wet dirt off.

"Hold it," said Bunny. "Do you speak English?"

The little guy started to move off, but Bunny grabbed him, and now he did not let him go. The little guy was about the size of a large Chihuahua dog.

"Shore 'n beggorah," said the little guy.

"English," said Bunny.

"Damn!"

"That's better," said Bunny.

"I mean it. Damn!"

"Damn what? I got you out of the hole. What were you doing in the hole, anyway?"

"I am not obliged to tell you that. You were just lucky."

"*I* was lucky? *I* was lucky! Hah, you are one lucky leprechaun, buddy."

"We don't use that word. It's demeaning. How would you like to be called Lefty?"

"I *am* called Lefty."

"Well, we are called the Little People."

Bunny hung on tight to the Little Person, knowing that he would scamper away if he could. The little person had a little white beard and a bit of a tummy, but he looked fit. He cursed, it seemed to Bunny, in his own language, and then said damn a few more times in English.

"Why do you claim that *I'm* the lucky one?" asked Bunny Watson, who had not used that word to describe himself over five baseball seasons.

"Ah, you are a foreigner. I can tell by your uncouth speech," said the little person. "Nevertheless, I am bound by a law older than that crumbled church over there, to tell you the rules. If you manage, through some incredible stroke of good fortune, to nab one of us and hold on, we must reward you."

"I like it," said Bunny. "But don't call it luck. It's skill. Years of conditioning and sacrifice have paid off."

"Oh, don't give me that sacrifice business. You sound like an Olympic athlete."

Bunny thought of stuffing this cranky little bugger back into the hole, but he was curious, and he *was* a fan of all things Irish.

"Okay, what about the reward? It had better have nothing to do with chocolate bars."

"Traditionally, you will be wanting me to show you where my pot of gold is hidden. I'll be the laughing stock of the Little World from Athlone to Kildare."

Bunny snorted.

"I don't need your gold. I'm a bonus baby."

"Go n-ithe an cat thú is go n-ithe an diabhal an cat!"

Bunny squeezed.

"English!"

"All right. No gold. What do you want instead of gold, my fine young foreign moron?"

"Well, last summer I went four and eighteen."

The 1962 Vancouver Mounties were not a powerhouse, but they played one of the most interesting seasons in the history of the Pacific Coast League, what with George Bamberger's shirt pocket radio and the UFO. Maybe we will get to the UFO later.

Bamberger was the long-time ace for the Mounties, of course. He was one of those guys, like Lefty O'Doul, who preferred to stay in the nice climate of the Pacific Coast League, so when the Vancouver franchise was passed from Baltimore to Milwaukee to Minnesota, and all the other players moved on, Bamby just stayed in town. On opening day, Bamberger used his 80 mph fastball and his smarts to down Tacoma. Then the Mounties lost two games, and the stage was set for their number four starter, Bunny Watson.

It was not an auspicious start. The sky was blue, and there was a light breeze, but it was not warm enough to make you sweat in your sweatshirt. Bunny had his fastball working, and his slider was on the verge of sliding. In the seventh inning he was behind 6-5, and working slowly, or as they say around ballparks, slow. He saw a right-handed person whose name he had not yet learned getting loose in the Mounties' bullpen down by the left field foul pole. That was just enough to get him through the seventh with no further damage, but his arm felt as if someone had injected it with mercury. If Jack McKeon asked him whether he had another inning in him, he would be honest with him.

He was due up third in the bottom of the seventh, so chances were that Jack was going to yank him, anyway. As fate would have it, he was fidgeting around in the on-deck circle when Julio Becquer banged a one-out double into the gap. Now, Bunny was a .083 lifetime hitter in the minors, so he was already walking back to the dugout when Julio performed an unnecessary stand-up slide at second. The guy who hit for him, Chuck Weatherspoon, nearly lost every item of clothing he was wearing when he swung at the first pitch, lofting the horsehide (as it still was in those days) high into the spring air. The center fielder knew just where it was going to come down, as center fielders, though not holding degrees in physics, seem to do, and headed for the fence.

He ignored the warning of the warning track, and leapt high against the painted plywood, his raised glove touching it just a foot below the spot where the baseball bounced off. The entire list of Pacific Coast League historians and fans regrets that there were no television cameras in Capilano Stadium, no slow-motion replay, no recording whatsoever. The centerfielder was going at a terrific rate, and when the baseball came down off the fence, it hit him on the top of his head, apparently, and his momentum propelled it right over the wall for a two-run homer.

The unnamed right-hander pitched two lovely innings of relief, and Bunny Watson, at 1-0, had his first winning record in three years.

The Vancouver papers had a good time describing the wonder, and the morning paper even printed a photo of the outfield, with a dotted line illustrating the course of the mighty blow. This was in 1962, remember, before the Vancouver papers decided that hockey and football should fill the sports pages during baseball season.

Less than a week later Bunny was working the mound in Spokane, where the air was already Inland Empire hot, and often filled with dust going around in circles. He was not overpowering the Indians, but after seven innings his arm felt only a little bit heavy, and his fastball was still veering off in some unpredictable direction ten feet in front of the plate. When your slider is not sliding all that much, it is nice to have some action on your heater. In any case, the Mounties and the Indians were deadlocked at five when Bunny came to bat in the seventh, a man on second and one out. He was hitting .000 on the season, with no other offensive stats.

But somehow, somehow, he got the fat part of the bat on a big fat fastball that didn't fast. This luck eventuated in a ground ball that slowed down dramatically in front of the second baseman. This fellow headed in practiced fashion toward the spheroid, but managed only two steps before falling on his face. The shortstop then scampered after the ball, which had almost come to a stop, but he too fell on his face.

The runner who had been on second was rounding the bag at third, when the pitcher fell on his face after one step toward the ball. Bunny was safe at first, dancing around, waving his arms, threatening to stretch his single into a double. He could have made it too; no one had picked up the ball.

The Indians mounted, as they say, a threat in the bottom of the ninth, but the young right-hander came in with one out and two on, and struck out the last two volunteers at the plate. Bunny was 2-0 on the season, ahead of George Bamberger in the win column.

You'd have to say that luck had a lot to do with it. Bunny was not exactly mowing them down, and his ERA was nothing to write home–or Minneapolis–about. Something similar was happening in his love life. She was not a Baseball Annie–in fact, until meeting Bunny Watson, she had never been to a professional ball game. Corny as it was, they met in front of the monkey cage at Stanley Park. The monkeys had a cage in front, and an island out back, rocks and trees and monkey stuff surrounded by a little lake of salt water in which the seals swam. When she walked from the glass front of the cage around to the seal part, he just plain followed her. Her name was Linda, of course, this being 1962, and she did not at all mind having a milkshake at the White Spot on Georgia Street.

She did come to the ballpark now, at least on the nights when Bunny was starting, and she brought her friend Marilyn with her, because it would have looked a little funny, sitting there in the grandstand all alone. Bunny told her that she and Marilyn should not sit in the box seats near the dugout. He didn't want anyone to get the wrong idea.

So the night after the day on which the Ranger 4 spacecraft crashed into the moon, she saw the notorious skunk play. Bunny was pitching his best game of the season, actually, and managed a complete game shutout against the San Diego Padres, the best-hitting team in the league. The Padre pitcher was no slouch himself that evening, and lost a 1-0 game due to a spot of poor luck mixed with controversial umpiring. In the bottom of the eighth Jim Snyder, the Mounties' number seven hitter, rapped a line drive just fair down the right field line. Snyder was just slowing down around second, when he caught sight of McKeon waving frantically in the coach's box back of third. So off he went, and around third he tore, and slid beautifully across the plate.

The ball was still lying on the dewy grass just a foot or so inside fair territory and twenty feet short of the fence. The Padres' right fielder was fifty feet farther into fair territory, waving his arms and kicking his feet. Standing on four feet right next to the ball, and sniffing at it with its long nose was a confident animal with lovely black fur with two white stripes along its length.

The San Diego manager and coach jumped up and down in front of the chief umpire for half an hour. They maintained that it should have been a ground rule double. The umpire avoided stepping on the caps that had been flung to the ground and repeated his opinion that there was no such ground rule regarding polecats. It may have seemed offensive, he ruled, but it was not interference.

Bunny breezed through the top of the ninth, and his record was 4-0.

Linda agreed that it would be wasteful to continue paying the rent on two apartments. Hers was close to the hospital where she supervised the kitchen, so he moved his small wardrobe in and started making friends with the mynah bird in its cage on the balcony.

He went to Seattle in her car instead of the team bus. They got their own hotel room, and she registered as "and Mrs." That was how they did things in those days. They saw just about everything there was to see in Seattle, and as game time approached he kept looking into the stands at Sick's Stadium, until he saw her abundant blonde hair and she waved at him. He took a lot of ribbing from his teammates, but that was easy to put up with. He was in love with a perfect woman and his won-lost record was at 5-0.

He beat the Rainiers 7-6 because an eighth inning two-out line drive bounced off his gluteus maximus into the bare hand of Bob Meisner, his second baseman, while the latter was falling to the ground as a result of trying to change direction, as the would-be tying run crossed the plate, and because a ninth-inning sacrifice bunt was stepped on by the would-be tying runner, causing his own put-out and converting the bunt into a single.

Bunny Watson had never been 6-0 in his life, not even as a sandlot pitcher in Boise. He did like the feeling, no doubt about that, but he was beginning to feel a little nervous. Of course he was thinking, as you are, about the leprechaun. He was a country boy from Idaho–of course he sort of believed in that sort of thing. He would never walk under a ladder or wear number 13. And he knew very well that normally an Irishman is nearly as big as a regular person.

Another thing he had never been in his life was so lucky in his love life. He knew that the Little Person had not said anything about his love life, but maybe these things always came as a package. Maybe he should have taken the pot of gold. No, he might have been able to put up with a so-so season, but could not imagine life without Linda.

"Would you love me if I was zero and six?" he asked her.

"Of course, dopey. I was nuts about you before I even knew the infield fly rule," she said.

"Dopey!" said the mynah bird.

So it went. Linda seemed to love him more and more. When he went on a long road trip that started in San Diego and proceeded northward, she waited for his return in their home that was just about exactly halfway between St. Vincent's Hospital and Capilano Stadium. When she had a day off and he had a night game, they would often enjoy a picnic at Queen Elizabeth Park, throwing bread crusts to the mallards that made large vees in the rock-ringed ponds. Once he saw a hole that must have been dug by some park animal, and imagined tiny humanoid legs sticking out of it.

Meanwhile his season proceeded steadily, from promising to good to miraculous. His ERA was more than a tad above the league average, but even reporters in other cities began to speculate about a season with no losses. In mid May he was pulled from an error-filled game in which he had fallen behind the Salt Lake City Bees nine to one, but in the top of the ninth the usually weak-hitting Mounties rallied for eleven runs, and his loss was changed to a no-decision. Bunny felt a little funny about that one. He felt as if maybe he had *deserved* a loss.

In fact, from then on he felt as if he kind of *wanted* to lose a game, and here is why: Bunny Watson may have been a bonus baby, and he may have tried to look unbeatable on the mound, but he was one of those rare ballplayers who just love the game. Most ballplayers love *playing* the game, but Bunny loved the game for itself. The difference is a little like the difference between a baseball spectator and a baseball fan. A spectator gets all excited about a game made out of home runs and errors, a game that finishes 17-15. A fan likes a game that is 1-1 going into the ninth inning, with both starters still in. A fan is a person who would never reach down and grab a baseball that was in play and then hold it up high and look around for praise.

So Bunny Watson did not like skunks in the outfield and infielders falling on their faces. One day, when they were shopping on West Broadway, he walked under a ladder. Linda gave him a look but she didn't say anything. A few days later he spilled the salt on purpose and did nothing about it. She figured that he was just feeling the pressure of leading the league in victories.

"You were a bonus baby," she told him, and gave him a nice neck rub right there at the table. "There was a reason they gave you all that money. They knew what you were capable of."

"Hey, you want to make a bet? I'll bet you ten bucks they don't hang Adolph Eichmann."

"Heh! Why don't you bet that you'll beat the Beavers tonight?"

"I'm not due to pitch till day after tomorrow," he said.

"You're on. Ten bucks," she said.

He could see what she was up to, and she could see that he could see, and if he were to lose those ten bucks to her, as he surely would, it would be worth it.

"I'm getting to love you," he said. "I can't believe my luck."

It was the night of May 28, 1962, and you could look it up in the May 29 Vancouver *Province,* or the *Flying Saucer Review,* for all I know. The game was interesting even without the celestial fireworks toward the end. The Mounties and the Beavers, two squads with .240 team batting averages, got through the regulation nine innings without getting a runner past second base. Portland's Dante Figueroa had given up four hits, and the home team pitcher Dagoberto Cueto, one of five Cubans on the roster, had given up six hits to the visitors.

Both teams got through the tenth without incident, and there must have been a lot of real fans in attendance, because it can get cool in late May around ten at night in Vancouver. That is to say, most of the 660 witnesses were still in their seats. Forty-three of them were in possession of small containers of alcohol derived from grain.

Señor Cueto strode, as they say, out to the mound for the top of the eleventh. It was past 10:30, and the air temperature was 41° F, about 40 degrees below the temperature in Havana. He walked a Beaver. He walked a second Beaver. There were none out. Everyone in the dugout was wearing a thick jacket. It was 10:40. From then until 10:45, according to the Vancouver *Sun*, Capilano was lit up by an unearthly light.

Here are some of the things the frightful object was called: "a flaming airliner," "a burning satellite," "an off-course rocket," "a comet," and "a flying saucer."

The ballplayers took to their heels, and the six hundred folks in the stands ran for the exits. All over the city automobiles were banging into each other as drivers stuck their heads out windows. Here is what a lot of farmers and retired people in the outlying districts were thinking: "that was no meteor–someone was flying that damned thing, and it wasn't any higher than four hundred feet." Around Boise, Idaho five minutes later, people raised shotguns and rifles and opened up at the monstrous thing.

But as we know, the show must go on, the game is not over until the last man is out, etc. After a half hour of big eyes and agitated footsteps, the umpires waved the Mounties and the Portland runners back onto the field. Ron Debus left one of his bats in the on-deck circle and walked up to the plate. Everyone was set to go, two on, none out, top of the eleventh.

But there wasn't any pitcher. Jack McKeon sent the batboy and the clubhouse boy and his second string catcher to look everywhere for Bert Cueto, but it was no use. The six foot four inch 170 pound righthander from San Luis was nowhere to be found. He had either been somehow abducted by the UFO or he had a bad reaction to flaming saucers. His civilian pants and shirt were hanging on a peg in the Mounties' dressing room, but he would not be around to deal with those two base runners and Ron Debus.

The 400 fans who had come back and arranged themselves among the best seats were starting to holler suggestions. The umpires talked among themselves, then ordered McKeon to get a chucker out there or forfeit the game. McKeon looked down his bench and outside the end of the dugout, where the reliefers were sitting on kitchen chairs. No one looked back at him. All their arms were stiff. They would warm up on a night when there were no fiery objects overhead. Except for Bunny Watson. Bunny knew that he was scheduled to start the day after tomorrow, so he gave Jack a smile.

"Okay, give me an inning, Watson," said McKeon.

Bunny couldn't believe his ears, but he picked up his glove and clacked his way up the dugout steps. Under these special circumstances, the umpires were willing to give him more than the standard seven warm-up pitches. He was feeling a kind of low-level exhilaration. If he was going to give up an extra base hit and allow those runs in, they would be Bert's responsibility. If this extra and unexpected work caused some trouble during his regular turn, he might actually lose a game and feel a great deluge of relief.

He threw five fastballs and four sliders to his catcher and said he was ready. He looked at his catcher's face behind the mask as the latter made his throw to second. He thought he looked a little Irish. Well, Joe McCabe. Probably an Irish name.

He got Debus on the infield fly rule. Then Jay Hankins fouled out. Then Bill Kern flied to deep right. Three pitches.

In the bottom of the eleventh the Mounties scored the only run they needed on a two-base error and a dying quail that the second baseman heroically but tragically dived for.

Bunny got the win without breaking a sweat, and he wished that he could give it to Bert Cueto, wherever he was.

By the time of the All-Star Game in Portland July 10, Bunny's record was 14-0, with an ERA of 5.45. If it had not been for the woebegone Spokane Indians, the Mounties would be in last place. They trailed the league in batting, they were second to last (Spokane) in attendance, and in fact no one except the executives in Minneapolis knew that after the 1962 season the Mounties would be out of the league for two years. George Bamberger would be coaching for McKeon at Omaha the following year, but would go 12-12 in 1962. None of the other pitchers was anything to write home about, whether San Luis or Little Rock. In the all-star game Bunny started and got knocked out of the box in the first inning. But when Bunny got to 17-0 at home against Hawaii, there was a reporter from *Sports Illustrated* in town to do an interview to be accompanied by a few black and white photographs.

"To what do you attribute your amazing run?" the reporter asked, showing the acuity that got him a job with the premier sport magazine.

"Luck of the Irish," said Bunny.

"You're Irish?"

"No. My grandfather changed his name from Wojcik to Watson. My cousin John Wojcik is playing a little in the Kansas City system."

"Have the Twins said anything to you? I mean, they are not exactly pitching rich these days."

"They're looking for young guys with ERAs under 4.00. That's what I've heard."

"Can we get a picture of you on the balcony with the crow?"

"It's a mynah bird. Can you get Linda in the picture?"

"One more question. What size shoes are those?"

All through July and August there were big league scouts in Cap Stadium whenever Bunny was due to start. They were all armed with radar guns, and could be seen shaking or slapping them after Bunny had really got behind one. His fastball was still flying off in every direction, but opposing hitters were making a living off his changeup.

Bunny was more and more a creature in conflict. He knew there was something fishy about his marvelous season, and as a faithful baseball fan he was tempted to walk ten batters in a row, or toss in nothing but batting practice pitches. But he was also a competitor, and he knew that if he threw a game, he would be doing just as stinky a disservice to the great game. He could *hope* like crazy that the Tacoma cleanup hitter might get ahold of one but he had to put that ball on or just off the corner of the strike zone. Meanwhile, away from the park he "accidentally" broke a mirror, went in search of road-crossing black cats, used a single match to light three friends' cigarettes, and stepped on every crack in the sidewalk. He quit doing that when his mother wrote him from Boise about her back problems.

He read every book and article he could find about leprechauns. Most of them said that leprechauns were only legendary or mythical creatures, and most of them mentioned pots of gold. He read James Stephens's novel *The Crock of Gold,* but Stephens didn't know anything about minor league baseball. One Saturday afternoon he had just about stopped worrying about anything, because Linda was walking around the apartment in nothing but a Vancouver Mounties cap. He was thinking about getting out of his chair, but then he recognized the song she was humming. It was "How are things in Gloca Mora?" He felt as if something had gone shooting by and he had just missed it. When he looked at Linda again she was walking away, sad and dreamy there.

What would she do if he got called up to Minnesota? She had a good job, a really nice apartment with a view of the mountains, and a mother and father living in Burnaby. What would she do in Minneapolis or St. Paul, especially when he was on the road? He almost dreaded the phone call from the Twins. But on the other hand, which in his case would be the right, he felt as if his 18-0 record was worth at least a phone call.

He gave some really hard thought to the conflicting sources of guilt and potential shame. Winning every game because of a supernatural hex was not, well, was not *baseball*. But losing a game on purpose was actually crooked. He was not a Black Sock. But he was not a Green Sock, either. He decided that he would do what he could about this perfect record. One thing he did not want was to be immortal because of that big zero. If he could lose one game the PCL record book would be besmirched, but at least the average baseball fan in the east would probably never hear about the 1962 Mounties and their big-footed miracle man and all that.

He decided that he would throw his first chance at twenty wins. On the third of August in Hawaii he won his nineteenth game when an easy fly ball bounced off outfielder Stan Palys's chest and then resisted his frantic attempts to pick it up and throw it. "Run, run!" his teammates were hollering at Ted Sadowski, who did not get a chance to do that very often. Fall down, fall down, whispered Bunny inside his head.

Which is exactly what he did while getting off the plane in Salt Lake City four days later. McKeon had told him that he was going to start against the Bees that night. "What bad luck," said Jack, and wondered why he was getting such a big smile off his ace lefthander in his Mormon hospital bed. Next day they sent Bunny to Vancouver, where he spent three days eating the hospital food that his sweetheart had approved way back before the season opener, then three weeks sitting in an easy chair with his foot up on a pile of pillows.

"Dopey!" said the mynah.

But Linda had something nicer to say. "There are some interesting treatments I thought of while you were in the hospital," she said. "In fact, I was already thinking of them when you were in Hawaii," she said. "So now I am thinking: what better time than now to show you what I have been mulling over?"

"Mulling?"

He got back into uniform on September first, and threw in the bull-pen to get his arm up to snuff. The main problem was making his big step, coming down on his leg, and torquing his body. His timing was all haywire at first because he flinched involuntarily when his right leg was getting ready to take the weight of his body just as the ball was leaving his left hand at 93 mph. Luckily, the Mounties played their last three series at home, against Portland, Salt Lake City and Spokane. He could work out his own timetable, throw as much as he felt able to do. One night he borrowed McKeon's radio receiver and stuck it inside his jersey. He tuned in CKWX and listened to Bobby Vinton and Neil Sedaka.

Finally, he told the skipper that he was ready to start, and on September fifth he took the mound against the Bees. It had been a few years since anyone had won twenty games in a PCL season, so there were lots of guys in hats in the stands, some with radar guns, others with wire-bound note-books. There were also a bunch of young goons in Section 10, shouting in unison, singing loudly, throwing soft things at one another, getting off hilarious comments that no one could understand. These were university students, back in town after a summer of rigorous work in forests and packinghouses. One of them was a young George Delsing, who was wearing a terry-towel head-covering complete with long rabbit ears, an homage, one was supposed to understand, to Bunny Watson.

Neither he nor anyone else in the crowd, not even Linda Krauss, knew that Bunny intended to lose this game. In the first three innings, though, he was a bonus baby grown up. His fastball was skittery, and his slider was a hell of a surprise. The Bees batted nine men in the first three innings. No one would ever guess that this hurler was not out for champagne. In those three innings the Mounties batted twelve men, and had got two hits, one of them a single up the middle by Bunny.

After six innings it was 1-0 in favour of the home team, and the Bees had two lousy little singles. McKeon sat beside Bunny and spoke to him without taking his eyes off the field.

"Your first game back. You ready to call it a night?"

"I feel like Satchel Paige, Jack. Got an arm made of rubber and gold."

"I'll talk to you after seven," said McKeon.

After seven it was still 1-0 for the home team, and Bunny was looking for his chance. Whoever was in charge of the PA system had played "How are things in Gloca Mora" between innings. It had to be a coincidence, but time was running out. Jack might pull him at any time. In the eighth inning he threw four pitches in the dirt. He refused to look toward the dugout or the bullpen. At the end of eight it was 1-0, and he was closer to running than to walking when he assumed his place on the mound. He had breezed right by his manager. There was a righthander in the pen, up and throwing.

Ninth inning—it was his last chance to avoid that 20-0 record. The Salt Lake City Bees were a Cubs' affiliate, but there was a lot of oomph in that lineup, and its main show was up in the ninth. Walt Bond started the inning off with a sharp line drive single to left. This is my chance, thought Bunny. He pitched carefully to the slugging first baseman Tony Washington, and walked him on five pitches. Max Alvis, who had 25 home runs, surprised everyone by laying down a sacrifice bunt, and then shocked them by beating the throw to first, mainly because third baseman Julio Becquer said something loud in Cuban twice before picking up the ball.

Okay, there were three baserunners and no outs. Jack McKeon was actually standing outside the dugout, staring hard at the mound, but Bunny would not look his way. In the stands, Linda had her sweater pulled up over her eyes. George Delsing shouted, "Now you got them right where they want you, Bunny," a line he had used more than once before. No one, though, could hear him clearly, there was such a noise in the stands. A batch of Canada geese flew low over the outfield, headed vaguely southward. Jack pushed his head forward and stared harder. Bunny looked off toward Little Mountain. Those were his baserunners on those bases, so even that young guy with no name would have to have supernatural help to get his starter off the hook this time. A grin went up the side of his face opposite to the side that McKeon could see.

Now at least Salt Lake's three .300 hitters were done. Their batting order was all downhill from here. Well, the next batter was La Vern Grace, who was batting .296. He was a man of mystery, as they say. He had made the team as a walk-on halfway through the season, and would disappear from sight a week after its end. This was the guy Bunny would sacrifice to the honour of the game.

He could have just thrown the ball fifteen feet over the catcher's head, but the competitor in him would not allow such a big margin. Bunny did his best to avoid thought, and before he knew it, the count was 3-2. Delsing turned to the guy standing beside him in Section 10 and shouted: three on, a 3-2 count, the next pitch is always a foul ball."

Okay, Bunny decided to make this pitch good and ambiguous. He went high and in, not exactly a beanball, but up enough and in enough to make a married man pee. It was his famous fastball with the tail. It started off looking like a strike, and then veering toward La Vern's left eye. La Vern tried to swing and fall on his ass at the same time.

What happened then took less time than this is going to take to tell you what happened then. First the baseball came into contact with a bat that was being moved three directions at once. Then the baseball travelled in a very slight arc to a spot midway between second base and the spot that the shortstop, in this case Jose Valdevielso, normally will occupy.

Señor Valdevielso reached up with his glove and caught the ball, retiring Mr. Grace, and a few steps later touched second base with his left shoe, thus putting out Mr. Washington, who could not get back fast enough, then kept running until he had reached Mr. Alvis, who had fallen down in his attempt to stop his progress toward second and attempt to return to the bag where he belonged. Jose V. reached down and tapped Max's leg with his glove.

Actually, this all happened about like this: You're Out! You're Out! You're Out!

Then Jose realized what he had just done. An unassisted triple play. Then Bunny realized what had happened. He was twenty and nothing. One by one the Mounties figured it out, and raced toward Valdevielso to jump on him and give him a congratulatory squeeze. All except their winning pitcher, who hung his head and walked as fast as he could toward the dugout and the dressing room behind it. There were two pictures in the *Sun* next day: one showed ballplayers in a pile, the other a non-celebrating walker. The caption suggested that the latter was in shock.

All that day the telephone rang in the apartment, and every time Bunny picked it up, the mynah bird said, "Hello?"

"Here's what I can't figure out," said Bunny, when Linda came home from work. "I get about a hundred calls since six this morning, and not one of them is from the Twins. While I'm at it, I also can't figure out how come they didn't call me up a month ago."

"It *is* odd, isn't it?" Linda replied. "I mean they're going to finish second."

He could not help smiling. She was keeping track of the American League standings. A year ago she had probably never heard of the Minnesota Twins. He felt lucky in love.

"Maybe," she said, "the Twins just never heard about what you have been doing this season."

"Or what's been done *to* me."

"Ah, that's crazy. The whole world knows, don't they?"

"Unless this is all a dream."

"So *I'm* dreaming too?"

"Maybe *you* are a dream."

Now he was getting a little scared.

"You know, I won't believe the numbers till I read the record books five years from now. And I *am* glad to be 20-0. I would rather be 20-0 than 4-18. But I would rather be, I don't know, 14-7. I kind of wish that I had taken the pot of gold instead."

The evening of September 9 would see the last Mounties game in Vancouver until 1965, and the last outing on the mound for their astonishing pitcher, Bunny Watson. The visitors were the cellar-dwelling Spokane Indians, who had already lost 96 games, and were not expecting to do much against Mr. Perfect. Bunny was thinking what the hell, the Russians have agreed to send missiles to Cuba, and we could all be ashes in another few weeks, we and all our records. He was just going to use his fastball all night, and see what happened.

There was a towel over something in his locker. Oh boy, his teammates were pulling something. But when he gingerly removed the towel, this is what he saw: a miniature kettle pot with one gold coin inside. He grinned while getting dressed. He put the coin in his pants pocket for luck. Then he grinned while taking his warm-up pitches. Then he went out and pitched nine innings and got whacked by the Indians 8-0.

He was still grinning when he joined his fiancée in the players' parking lot.

"What is your real name?" he asked her.

"Iris," she said.

In the Event of a Five-way Tie for a Division Title

While unlikely, the potential for a five-way division title tie at the end of the regular season does exist. Major League Baseball needs to be prepared, so here is the official tie-breaking rubric:

Each team will have a chance to play for the division title, and if applicable, the wild-card.[1]

Team "A" plays Team "E." The winner will be deemed Team *x*.
Team "B" plays Team "D" The winner will be deemed Team *y*.
Team *y* plays Team "C." The winner of that game will play Team *x*.

The winner of *y*/"C" vs. *x* will be awarded the Division Title. If the wild-card spot is still in dispute, the four remaining teams will play each other in a single-elimination bracket-style tournament triple-header, as follows:

Team "A" -   - Team "B"

_____ vs. _____

Team "D" -   - Team "C"

Determining which teams will be A,B,C,D,E:

Head-to-head records will be consulted first. If these are also identical,[2] teams will choose one player via secret ballot to complete a timed, supervised general knowledge exam.[3] The test scores will determine choosing order.

In the event of a tie between exam grades (for example, if Pedro Martinez and John Smoltz split their Victorian literature scores) the deadlocked players will compete in a modern pentathlon at Miller Park in Milwaukee. The modern pentathlon consists of épée fencing, pistol shooting, 200 m freestyle swimming, a show jumping course on horseback, and a 3000 m cross-country run.[4] The winner's club will choose which designation (A, B, C, D, E) it wants among the remaining options.

If there is still no clear winner, the world championship will be awarded to the New York Yankees.

---

[1] In order to reduce travel time, the commissioner may select a neutral site equidistant from all teams' home cities. If no appropriate stadium exists at the site, one will be constructed.

[2] Such was the case with the 2005 Red Sox and Yankees. However, as both teams were assured a playoff berth, no tiebreaker was necessary.

[3] Given the international make-up of today's Major Leagues, an exam entirely in English would be unfair. Therefore, the test will be in Esperanto.

[4] Invented by the Baron Pierre de Coubertin, founder of the modern Olympic Games, the modern pentathlon was created to simulate the experience of a 19th century cavalry soldier behind enemy lines: he must ride an unfamiliar horse, fight with pistol and sword, swim, and run.

Reflections on the Game by Red Anderson: Age 116, Hero of the Dead-ball Era and the World's Oldest Living Baseball Player.

I was discovered when I was a boy working in the family butcher shop in Pittsburg. I was eight years old, and had been working full-time for five years. Before that it was part-time, 60 hours a week.

I'll always remember that day. I was swinging a cow's leg at an Irish; would you believe that drunken Paddy was in asking for a job? Fred Clarke, the Pirates' manager, happened to be in the store that day buying his weekly suckling pig and admired the way I was able to clobber that potato-eating Mick. Once he had stopped laughing, he asked me if I had ever played base-ball. Sure! I said. After all, he was talking to the four-time Rock-Ball champ of my block.

Rock-Ball was a Pittsburg game exactly identical to stickball only instead of a ball you used a rock, and instead of a stick you used your arm. This was during the Great Stick Famine of 1899, after all.

The Pirates bought me from my parents for 11 dollars. I say, that was a lot of money back then! It allowed them to buy an auto-mobile and a China-man to replace me at the store. A drunk Crimean War veteran who played the Pirates mascot became my legal guardian.

We were paid 9 dollars a month, plus an extra opium ration if we were on a winning streak.

Red isn't my Christian name, no. I was born Percival Aloysius Anderson, but got the name "Red" after it came out that my mother had once kissed an Apache boy.

Even though the club owned its own hot-air balloon, travel remained slow and difficult. As a result, we would routinely play quadruple or quintuple-headers, sometimes more. One August afternoon I pitched in six consecutive games, and caught for another two.

Oh yes, I played with all the greats. Ducky Wright. Spanky Donaldson. Matches Kilroy. Half-Face Brown (The other half having been kicked off by a Clydesdale prior to a game wherein he pitched a perfect game.)

People often ask me what Honus Wagner was like. I must admit that I never spoke to the man directly, having been raised to be ever distrustful of the crafty Dutchman.

Over my 18 year career, my pre-game regiment was always identical: I would sup on 4 roasted ducks, a half-dozen scrambled eggs, 14 bottles of stout, a capsule of Zulu blood (expensive!) and, of course, co-caine.

In 1908, I won the home-run title with a total of three dingers. I would have had four, but a donkey tied up in center-field caught the spheroid in its maw, robbing me! In those days, any beast present on the field was considered in-play. Rest assured, I promptly smote that wretched animal before the entire cheering crowd!

I was the first player to be personally endorsed by a company. During my third season, I struck a deal with Chesterfield Cigarettes which stipulated that I must always be smoking their product while on the field. Truthfully I credit much of my superlative career to the full-bodied toasted flavor of those silky-smooth Chesters.

Players today? Pish! Pussies, the whole lot!

Miss Scarlet, Number 21

Late start. Milkshakes on the way and night folds
onto the Astroturf
as we pile from the Boddy manor van.
There's my face in the field lights
just pre-night. Shining, moth white.
Before, I wore blue and the air
apes some sweatshirt I used to know.
But there is no mystery
here. The sky was broad and cleanish
and now is not.
Mustard, saucy in green. "Pass the pigskin."
Peacock: "Love, wrong game."
Sofa So Good is not a team we've know to forfeit.
And so Plum stirs tang. Spreads the plastic tablecloth
thin. And me in a slow circle
tossing bases to the dirt.
Green mutters when nervous, it's true. Now, in half light,
alone: "Batter up." White practicing.
Aims a bat, cuts air.

Fair Play

The window is painted shut
but I can crack it, sit down, and let loose
the holy-ish fury of much-practiced
Hot Cross Buns. And then? Well
just wait. I don't need to look,
can see in my mind's polished eye
third period gym's baseball game
pause. Together now: peek up.
Stunned? Try this on for size. Assembled,
my flute near as long as a baseball bat.
Third period, the chemical eyewash station a waste
of my fingers' talents, their nimble piccolo dance.
Much depends, mind, on how hard I can blow.
Baseball team's uniforms mere white, marching band rocks
blue. A moment, now, to savour the gold rick-rack trim.
Your bicep, yes. But have you seen me circular breathe?
I don't mind telling you that the flute I can take or leave,
but climb marching band for elevation, so as to see
this sordid world's smoother side.
In this life I neither bunt nor take the walk.
Friends, be aware. Life-wise, I'm stealing third.
Tuck run, oboe close to the hip.

My Life as a Major Leaguer

I met my best friend, Jim Schenz, when we were three years old, growing up in a white bread suburb of Cincinnati, Ohio. Among other peculiarities, he found it impossible to pass a puddle without inspecting its contents at some length. He eventually became a marine biologist. I, on the other hand, have always been puzzled by people who always knew what they wanted to be when they grew up. There were and are plenty of things I want to do, but I never really wanted to *be* anything–still don't, really–except a Major League baseball player.

I'm pretty sure that Jim Schenz was, if not the cause, at least the occasion for this desire to burst forth. For Jim, Huck Finn to my more staid Tom Sawyer, used to mysteriously disappear for months at a time only to reappear each Autumn with traveler's tales of exotic locales–strange places with improbable names like Chicago, St. Louis, and Pittsburgh. Pittsburgh, he told me, with what I innocently believed to be hyperbole, was entirely covered in thick, gritty coal dust. After a few years I came to understand these absences–his father, Hank Schenz, was a ballplayer. A Major League ballplayer. You could look it up.

He was, alas, a rather marginal major leaguer, a player who managed to hang around the Big Leagues in a part-time role for a few years, accumulating in the end a lifetime total of 508 ABs–one season's worth for a full-time player.

By the time I started to pay attention to Major League baseball, late in the 1955 season, Schenz's brief major league career had ended, and he was now a minor league manager. This is a typical career move for intelligent players with limited skills (i.e., players like Hank Schenz), and many of the finest major league managers were originally players of just this type. But by the late fifties Hank was out of baseball altogether. (Possibly his failure to rise through the managerial ranks had something to do with a characterization of him I once saw in a baseball magazine.

The author of the article opined that "bench jockeys"–players who succeed in throwing opponents off their game by well-timed remarks about their manliness, ancestry, and personal hygiene–are rarely effective. In the entire century-plus history of the game only 3 or 4 men had figured out how to be so annoying as to visibly unnerve the opposition. Hank Schenz was said to be a master of the genre. Could they really mean Jim Schenz's dad? Well, uhhh... no comment, your honor.)

But I wasn't thinking much about Hank Schenz in the Mid-50s. I just played baseball every day and assumed I would be a Major Leaguer. The Jews (and some African cultures) say that when you're 13, you're a grownup. Well, maybe so. For, at 13, the first tiny cracks of adult rationality began to invade my hermetically sealed baseball fantasy world. There seemed to be a few problems. I could hit alright, but I was a lousy fielder–a really lousy fielder. I knew this, but most of the time I imagined my deficiencies could be corrected with the hard work and earnestness my parents and teachers claimed could solve any problem. However, I also couldn't really run very well. And let's face it, if you can't run very fast at 13, when will you be able to?

Somehow, though, I managed to overlook or at least repress these doubts for the next few years. But in 1959 I was 15. And Hank Schenz was 40. He now managed a fast-food restaurant, had grown a sizeable belly, and played softball once a week at the local park. And it was here in Chamberlain Park that I finally had my epiphany. Except for Hank, all the players in this league were guys between the ages of 18 and 25; and this 40 year-old, pot-bellied restaurant manager could run so much faster, throw so much harder, and hit the ball so much farther than anyone else that it seemed he must have just dropped in from the planet Krypton.

"Eventually," Kafka said, "enlightenment comes to the dullest." I finally got it; I wasn't good enough to play in the big leagues, and failing divine intervention (which I already knew wasn't coming), I never would be good enough.

Later that summer, during a pick-up game, I neglected to slide as I went into second base. The second baseman, trying for a double play, pivoted in an odd manner, and I intercepted his throw to first with my nose. That was it for the summer; during my convalescence, I started reading *Crime and Punishment,* and, well, it's all been pretty much downhill since then.

Except... once upon a time, many years later, I found myself with my friends Ron and Patricia endlessly circling Boston on the satanic Möebius Strip known as Route 128. As afternoon slowly ground down, traffic became more and more frenzied, No Vacancy signs flashed by in dreary profusion, and we sank deeper and deeper into *l'anomie des autoroutes.*

Finally, as the shades of evening drew on, we found ourselves before the gates of a motel–the Love Motel, as its glowing red neon letters proclaimed. The important thing, though, was that it had some available rooms. The room clerk seemed startled when we requested two separate rooms, but he hid his surprise with a show of professional briskness, and I was soon ensconced on my big heart-shaped waterbed. At this point I wanted nothing more from life than to dip into my stash of Diet Coke and maybe find a ballgame on the tube.

However, it was not to be; Ron knocked on my door and suggested that we take the enclosed walkway over the 128 and play some miniature golf. As we had already noted while getting out of the car, the golf course appeared to be populated with dinosaurs. While I had been bonding with my motel room, which contained all the important things missing from my life (wow! Air conditioning! Cable TV! A shower with sliding doors!), Ron had already scouted out the course and he explained to me that we would be required to hit the ball up the brontosaurus's tail, carefully guide it through the scales of a side-lying stegosaurus, and brave a rapacious tyrannosaurus rex by banking it off one of his massive hind legs. Incredibly, I found this prospect tempting. So off I went, to try my hand at dinosaur taming. But Ron whipped me badly. (Confession: except for baseball I've always been fairly pathetic as an athlete. In high school gym class, we played softball only briefly, a few times every Spring. I invariably hit a home run the first time up because the opposing outfielders naturally assumed that my baseball skills were of the same magnitude as my other athletic endeavors and positioned themselves as you would for a not-too-athletic eight year-old.)

As fate would have it, the mini-amusement park also had a batting range (not a cage–a batting range, like a golf driving range, with 100, 200, 300, and 400 foot signs so you could see how far you hit the ball. I never saw anything like it, before or since.) Ron suggested that we hit some. At that distant time (the early '80s) the pitches came from the same sort of practice machine sometimes used by professional ballplayers. This machine was called "Iron Mike," and it was not all that popular with the pros because Iron Mike was known to be very wild. The ball might be so far off the plate that it was impossible to hit–or it might come straight at your head.

I couldn't get this fact out of *my* head when Ron suggested that we select Mike's 90 mph pitches to hit against. (Mike had 3 speeds: 40 mph, 70 mph, and 90 mph.) Let me explain: 40 mph is the speed of the underhand softball pitches lobbed by the guy with a beer in his other hand at the company picnic. 70 mph is about the speed attained by a 13 yr. old Little League pitcher. And 90 mph is a Major League fastball. From the time it leaves the pitcher's hand (or chute, in Mike's case) a 90 mph ball takes approximately four-tenths of a second until it reaches the plate (or your head). I pointed out to Ron that our street shoes were rather slippery, which would hinder us if we needed to quickly get out of the way of one of Mike's errant pitches. And–there was no getting around it–we would have to dodge these wild throws with 40 yr. old reflexes.

We compromised; we would take alternate swings at Mike's pitches ($2.50 for ten pitches), and see how we fared. The 1st pitch, a chin high inside fastball, missed Ron by two or three inches and left him looking a trifle shaky. "Get out of the way, Ron," I said, and he did. And I did, too. We watched Mike's next pitch go right across the center of the plate. But neither of us got in the batter's box for the 3rd pitch. Or any of Mike's other 90 mph offerings. No, we huddled ignominiously (but safely, safely) off to one side while Mike served 'em up.

The entire debacle can't have lasted more than three or four minutes, but my humiliation was intense. It must feel like this to wash out of the Marines or to flunk second grade. However, Ron's *amour propre* had apparently been less affected. "Let's try the 70 mph pitches," he chirped.

He hung in there (as the pros say) and took his cuts, but he couldn't hit the 70 mph pitches either. But, to my utter delight, I discovered that I could. The bat still made that curious hollow "plonk" when the contact was good, and there was the same remembered sense of effortlessness or grace at the moment of contact–as though the ball was filled with some lighter-than-air substance. I began to hit line drives and long fly balls, one after another, and the next half hour or so passed in pure joy.

But, as we've been told, there are no second acts in American life; anyway, joy doesn't come at our summoning; so I never tried to repeat the experience. As long as I never swing a bat again, I can continue to believe I'm still a Major Leaguer; after all, as a great Yogi once said, "ninety percent of this game is half mental."

The Third Base Coach Touched Himself again

It was years later when I realized the Little League baseball coach was actually not a pedophile. Although there had never been any proof, it was something always hinted at and in the back of parents' minds–like an old bicycle in the back of the garage. I was twelve and serious about baseball and so were my teammates. The summer was wide open, to be filled with the kind of discipline which was forbidden in our school. Some of the parents thought two practices a day were too much but we, the West Side Tigers, loved it. We were all-stars after all.

The coach took photographs of the players and sold them back to their parents. I guess it was the nature of the photos which caused any red flags. There were the blow-ups of our swings, black and white glossies of a pitching stance, but also the changeroom shots, the candids. It was slightly odd as well that he was a bachelor who we felt obligated to call Mister. He was the only coach in the league who didn't go by his first name.

Every year the league had the kids sell raffle tickets to raise money. Every year the coach rallied the West Side Tigers together and reminded us of the prize for the team which sold the most tickets. An all-you-can-eat dinner at McDonalds. I stood outside liquor stores in my uniform accosting inebriated shoppers who thought I looked cute. The coach made me get the same haircut as everyone else on the team and I had to wear my uniform everywhere, as if a throwback to the early days of sport. If I had been older I'm sure I would have been expected to wear a suit on the off-days. I certainly didn't own a suit.

When I advanced to the older West Side leagues the coach would sometimes be the umpire. He was very decisive but fair. Ironically, and unjustly in my opinion, he once chastised me, his former player, when I sat in the stands wearing my uniform. Of course I was trying to flirt with Stacey, who had come to watch the game, but the former coach was jealous. Or so I thought. Now I realize he just wanted us to be invested in the game. By this time I had a new coach. He was an obese Harley driving man-boy who still lived with his mother. He knew his baseball but he was more of a drinking buddy than a father figure. Us players on the West Side Thunderbirds even called him by his first name. No Mister for Jesse. When Jesse got angry over a clumsy error it was hard to take him seriously. At one point he decided to get help. He introduced us to a young guy, not much older than me, who was an army reservist. He wore khakis and suddenly it was mandatory to do drills, then run through the thick bramble of the woods scratching our faces while listening to his army taunts. After practice some of us on the team went back to Jesse's mother's basement and the army reservist would drink a case of beer and punch holes in the walls. Coach Jesse exposed us to his porn movie collection. I held a pillow in my lap and said nothing.

I often said nothing. There was nothing to say. I was living for the three and one count where I knew I'd see a good pitch, one I could pull up the line, or drop over the infield for a base hit. At night I saw these pitches in my mind, saw the seams float in and felt my wrists curl at the exact moment, the smell of liniment, the sweet spot. I was the lead-off hitter since I was the fastest on the team and could steal bases. Often I would swing at the first pitch of the game, just to catch the other team off guard. When we got older the pitching became faster. The best teams would practice on pitching machines cranked up to maximum so when we played them I would be called in to pitch. I was the opposite of a pitching machine cranked up to maximum. I was a knuckle-baller.

Even in the Show it is unusual to go up against a knuckle-ball pitcher so I was downright exotic in our humble league. As the other team watched me warm up they could not contain their enthusiasm, since the ball lumbered across the plate like a baked potato due to my weak throwing arm. They assumed they would have a day of batting practice. Then, when the game started, I'd never throw a single fastball (or in my case a slow ball). They were flummoxed. Often enough for the Thunderbirds to win the game in a resounding upset. Once or twice their frustration led to a bench-clearing brawl. But that was also the big mouth of Spence, our go-to pitcher. He threw hard but often his arm would be like a piece of hamburger by the middle of the game. No stamina.

Malicious head-hunting pitches were the retribution for a second base spiking. Standing up for an honour, forgotten now. These were the stuff of the bench-clearing brawls. The largest came in the provincial tournament when we were playing for last place. The opposing pitcher came too far inside on Spence back in the third inning and now received the same treatment in kind. I was playing third. I reacted without thinking. When the batter rushed Spence our catcher gave chase and I was off my mark. I was later told the opposing third base coach, a bald man in his fifties, lunged at me and was tackled by the reliever who had been chewing spits in the dugout. The players met at home plate. Punches were thrown. I arrived in time to break it up. The game was delayed so that we could receive a lecture from the league commissioner about setting an example. I didn't know our league warranted a commissioner. Did he live with his mother too?

The last time I saw Spence he was night-pitching like a drunken mime. We had met at a party. We were both in town for the holidays. It was one of those holiday parties where you feel discombobulated with nostalgia and drink. Spence had kids now. Spence offered to drive me home. I couldn't tell if he was drunk but agreed anyway. I needed to get home. He took the long way. He passed by the old park where we had played Little League baseball. He parked the car. As we strolled in from the outfield Spence reminded me of that time in Duncan, when we were billeted together.

We were picked up at the community centre by a kid with a mullet who was a bit younger than us. His brother was in the pick-up outside with his mulleted buddies. We rode in the back of the truck. On the drive, beer bottles kept appearing out of the windows, flying at full speed into the drainage ditch. At the modest home on the edge of town, before the land became obviously rural, but not exactly suburbs either, there were no guardians. Spence and I were unsure what to think. We were being billeted without adult supervision. A few years later this would appeal to me but at the time I was frankly scared. What would become of us? Sure enough, after a big party that partly took place in the kitchen, the brother was hungover and it was touch and go whether we'd get to the field in time, but he came through. My parents were in the stands and when I casually mentioned that there was no chaperone, they insisted that I stay at the hotel with them. I was suddenly extremely embarrassed and asked that the issue be dropped and Spence and I continued for another two nights in the house of mullets. When the coach took pictures of the players with their billets I went to find the water fountain.

Although the night was threatening rain, Spence wanted to pitch and that's when I knew he was drunk. Tears rose to his eyes as he wiped the sand off the rubber with his toe. He needed me to take a swing. We were both lefties. He wound up, lifting his leg, and I noticed the fence in the outfield. When I had played there was never a fence. If the ball made it to the road it was a homer. If it bounced, a double. The fence seemed just out of reach. I couldn't believe I had never hit a homer. It seemed so easy to me now. I timed the swing perfectly and the air I displaced was legendary.

We walked the infield remembering double plays, epic Buckner blunders, the nicks and quality of the dirt. The grass had been replanted in our absence and many of the small indentations had been filled. We could barely fit in the space between the chain-link allocated for the dugout. Spence told me his marriage was over. Just like that. As I was trying to squeeze my ass into the dugout he told me the kids were too hard to control. Then he sprinted. He sprinted the bases as fast as he could all the while calling out the play by play. "He rounds second and the right fielder has bobbled the ball, he's come up with it, and here's the throw to third... but it's too high, into the fence, and he's trying for home." Spence slid into home plate. Slid, ruining his dress slacks, ripping them even. When I pointed out the rip to him he said, "It's worth it. I can always get another pair of pants but how often do I get to ding an inside-the-park home run?"

Back in McDonalds in my uniform. Eating all I could eat. I only ate hamburgers, never anything larger, like a Big Mac. I thought at the time that I was being crafty, pacing myself to be able to eat more, but now I realize that I never much liked meat. The other patrons thought my uniform was cute, but really they were enablers. The coach took our photos. Fries in our noses. Ketchup smiles. Our uniforms were freshly laundered, not even traces of the infield from an earlier game. We were dressing in our uniforms to eat, to ritualize our victory, replace it, engorging our acne scarred faces, sucking on straws, pulling the sugar ever deeper, while the parents wondered what ever happened to the negatives.

It turns out the army reservist had connections and he found himself a trainer for the National Junior team. I couldn't believe it. This guy? Sure he was tough and made us do drills, but what about all that wall punching? The porn? But then he asked me personally to try out. I was honoured until I got to the tryouts. They were at Nat Bailey Stadium and there were hundreds of guys. Almost all of them were bigger and older than me. They wore batting gloves! I tried out at third but was not familiar with a perfectly groomed field. This was the field where the

Vancouver Canadians played, the farm team for the Milwaukee Brewers. I never did get the connection, except maybe the beer. The Canadians had the same logo as the beer it was named after. I kept expecting a wayward bounce but the ball would smoothly and predictably roll under my glove. I had one of the faster running times but then in the hitting demonstration I was way behind the ball because I was nervous. No one seemed to care that I could throw a knuckle-ball. And no one has cared since then either.

When Spence left the darkened Little League field, he leaned over the new fence and pretended to catch a fly over the wall, but the gesture was one of a middle-aged man. At McDonalds Spence would eat more than anyone, but that was because he never bulked up on fries. He was into pure meat. And now all those adolescent Big Macs have decided to document their own history by becoming archeologically implanted on his waistline.

Spence had not been asked to try out for the National Junior team and therefore he resented me. At the tryouts we were all called together. The army recruit was in the stands drinking a beer and picking at the paint on the seat in front of him with a knife. "This is only the first day of tryouts," said one of the older trainers. "The following guys can come back tomorrow…" At this point he read a list of names from his clipboard. Trouble was he only read first names and there were over one hundred names of boys who would be returning. My common enough name was called four times! I assumed none of them referred to me and I didn't want to ask. I didn't want to find myself alone with the army recruit in a dark basement, a case of beer, a VCR, and a knife. I tried to tell Spence that baseball was all over for me but he was still resentful. True to my word, I never played again.

On the way back to the car in his ripped slacks, Spence asked me, "Remember the coach, how he was always taking photos of us?"

"Ya. So?"

"Turns out he was an artist."

"What do you mean?"

"He exhibited those photos, like ten years later. My aunt saw the review of the show in the paper."

"Oh that explains it," I said. "By the way, that inside-the-park homer would have been scored a triple with an error. Sorry."

As we left the diamond Spence started his car simply by pointing in its direction, as if by magic.

Crime Dog

It would be more than slightly inaccurate to say that I'm a fan of Fred McGriff. In reality, I hate him as a man and I hate him as a stoic slugger with one of the twenty-first century's truly great moustaches.

One evening in 1999, I was on a date with a high school Spanish teacher from Zephyrhills. We were at the West Shore Plaza Theatre waiting to see *Varsity Blues* when we had the dubious fortune of running into McGriff. He was attending the movie with his wife and two teenage daughters. My date Brenda and I were seated near the back of the theatre and the McGriffs chose the row of seats directly in front of us. Fred was wearing a black leather coat over a charcoal grey rib-knit sweater.

"Who is that lanky son of a bitch?" I said sarcastically to Brenda. I knew from the profile of the moustache that it was him. Fred McGriff, that cocksucker, in the flesh.

"I beg your pardon," she said.

"Nothing," I said. "You ready for a refill on your Fresca?"

"Is that who I think it is?" Brenda whispered.

"I'll be right back," I said. I grabbed my half-full soda cup and bolted toward the fire exit. By the time I realized I'd left my cell phone in the pocket of my sport coat in the theatre, the emergency exit door had slammed behind me and I was standing in a dark mall loading dock in Tampa, Florida.

I realize that fleeing the scene of a hot date and an acclaimed high-school football blockbuster on the account of a Major League Baseball star sounds like a strange thing to do, so let me explain. In 1984, when I was in my third semester at Dawson Junior College, I met Fred's younger brother Kenny at a fraternity Hallowe'en party. Kenny McGriff arrived at the party just before midnight with two girls from Chicago who'd flown in to visit him for the weekend. Kenny was a young recruit in his freshman year and he was already being touted as my primary competition for the second string catcher position on the varsity baseball team. Spring Training was still more than four months away, but Kenny was highly regarded, in my opinion, mostly because his older brother was a blue-chip MLB prospect.

That March, Kenny McGriff stole my second string catcher position less than two days into Spring Training, bumping me to bullpen catching duties for my final two years at Dawson. By the time the season started, he'd earned the starting catcher job, which he celebrated by safely reaching base in 12 of his first 14 at bats. Kenny developed an instant rapport with the pitching staff and he was named conference player of the month after he clubbed five home runs on our first three game road trip of the season, which, incidentally, I was not invited on.

In 1986, four months after I was cut from the varsity team following a shoving match with our bench coach, I saw Kenny at another off-campus house party. Not only was he the star of the baseball team that had just won its first league pennant in school history, but his older brother was an emerging slugger with the Toronto Blue Jays. Kenny was, more or less, the coolest guy an average college girl will ever meet.

To go into a lot of detail about what happened that night at the house party isn't really the point. I'm not going to say that what I did was justified, but my actions certainly weren't without provocation. Kenny never should have asked me if I knew how to catch a cold in front of my date, Cynthia Chang, and he never should have been making out with her in the hallway later in the evening. When the empty Milwaukee's Best bottle I threw hit Kenny in the left eye, and not between his shoulder blades, it was not only a shame, but a total fluke. The accidental nature of the toss seemed to be lost on a fairly large group of my former teammates because it wasn't long before they turned on me and put me in the hospital with, what I can only assume, was a thorough beating on the front lawn.

Kenny was in surgery for six hours to repair his retina and stitch his eyelid back together. Despite the best efforts in the emergency room, Kenny was never given medical clearance, nor had adequate vision to ever catch another pitch in Hawk Dawson Stadium.

I recovered from the assault fairly quickly but I was promptly expelled from Dawson Junior College for what the Dean cited in my hearing as, "unfathomable violence." Kenny didn't return to Dawson after his operation and rumours began circulating that he wasn't the star in the classroom that he was on the field. I tried to tell people that I had done Kenny a favour by ending his baseball career and opening his eyes, so to speak, to other opportunities. Unfortunately for me, by that time I didn't have too many friends and no one was overly interested in what I had to say. Kenny apparently moved back to Tampa where he got involved in a cushy inner-city youth baseball program. To my knowledge, he never had another at bat in a competitive baseball game.

So when I saw Fred in the West Shore Plaza Theatre that night, it's no secret why I wasn't keen on sticking around and being buddy-buddy with the man who was the catalyst for ruining my promising college life and whose brother ended my baseball career.

When I dialed my cell from a phone booth outside the theatre, I dishonestly explained to Brenda that I hadn't been feeling well and my dash to the back alley was a successful attempt to rid myself of the suspect chicken salad sub I had eaten too quickly at lunch. Brenda met me outside the theatre and was astonishingly understanding.

"I'm sorry we couldn't see the movie," I said. "I heard James Van Der Beek is amazing."

"It's alright," she said. "McGriff's aftershave was making me nauseous. Besides, I wasn't in the mood for a movie."

"What do you think about grabbing a steak?" I asked.

"Sure," Brenda said. "As long as you're confident your stomach can handle it."

We walked to the Applebee's in the mall parking lot across from the theatre. We ordered a pitcher of MGD, cheese bread and a pair of rib eye steaks.

Brenda and I met through a mutual friend we had in an Internet community for people interested in travel. Marco198 lived in Alberta and introduced Brenda and I when he realized we both lived in West Florida. The rest, as they say, was history. We exchanged a few e-mails and spoke on the phone twice. I figured we were becoming friends, but then suddenly I didn't hear from her for almost a month. Brenda explained her on-line absence as a result of work related travel, but I suspected it had to do with a boyfriend. When she finally replied to my fourth e-mail in two days near the end of that month, she agreed to meet me for a movie. And here we were. Two people on a movie date who were now waiting for cheese bread at Applebee's.

"So where were you on business?" I asked Brenda. "You know, being a teacher and all."

"I have to confess. I haven't been completely honest about that," Brenda said. "I was in Pennsylvania."

"Pennsylvania?"

"Yes," she said. "My son lives there. With his father and stepmother. I went there to spend some time with him. He'll be two in January."

"Sounds like a long story," I said.

"It is," she said. "Anyway, it looks like I might be able to take him for the summer. I'm off for nine weeks and his father is expecting another child any day now."

"Cool," I said. "What's his name?"

"Glen," she said.

"Glen? What an odd name for a baby. Glen."

"He's a beautiful child. I can't wait to introduce you." The Applebee's server delivered our cheese bread and offered fresh pepper.

"Glen," I muttered. "When did fresh pepper become so indispensable?"

Brenda said quietly. *"De modo que imprescindible."*

"Glen."

The truth was, I was thinking about McGriff. I was thinking about him watching *Varsity Blues* with his wife and daughters. I also thought about him playing first base and I imagined him phoning his brother from the clubhouse after he won the World Series with the Atlanta Braves. I imagined his saying something sentimental to Kenny, like it could have been him winning the World Series if it hadn't been for me, Olivier Jones, the deranged college bullpen catcher. I dipped my cheese bread in the spicy yogurt sauce and looked at Brenda. She was smiling.

"What do you say we spring for a bottle of *vino*," I said, picking up the drink menu from the condiment caddy.

"You bet," she said. "That would be nice with our main course." I like the way she described our steaks. Main course, it sounded sophisticated.

A lot of people would look at a pretty gal like Brenda and think about one thing, boning. But a lot of other people, myself included, would think about other things. They'd think about her hair and her beautiful voice. They'd admire her ability to speak more than one language and the lovely way she describes a meal. First course, second course, third course. It sounds so much nicer than cheese bread and rib eyes. Let's face it, she's a great woman. *Ella es una dama buena.*

"I think your ex-husband was a fool," I told her.

"We were never married," she replied. "We met at a Spring Break party in Daytona. I spent no more than two hours with him. I couldn't afford to take care of Glen on my own, so Brian temporarily took him back to Williamsport. We agreed that when I have the money to live in a nicer neighborhood and I have a boyfriend, Glen will come live with me."

"Would you look at these wine prices," I said, studying the wine card. "Jesus Christ, twenty-eight dollars for a Canadian Cab-Merlot."

"Let me look at that," Brenda said. "I'll choose a good one." I happily handed her the wine card. I know very little about wine aside from the fact that it comes in two colour options and among the world's great wine producers, Canadian wineries are probably as respected as their impotent national tennis program.

We had a great meal. Cheese bread, steaks, a "robust" Chilean Merlot. Brenda and I have been back to Applebee's many times since. Glen now lives with her and I in Tampa where we rent a two-bedroom condo. I've learned some Spanish vocabulary and I've learned to love Glen like he's my own son. I think, in Brenda's eyes, he is my son. She hasn't mentioned Brian's name since our first date and she indicated once that she doesn't plan on telling Glen about his real father when he gets older. From all accounts, it doesn't appear Brian will have any problems with this.

Brenda and I have season tickets to the Devil Rays where Fred McGriff played his final season in 2004. We took great pleasure in seeing him on the DL and unable to play most of the MLB season. We were also pleased to see him forced to retire at the end of that season, only seven home runs short of five hundred, a missed milestone I bet he and Kenny often discuss regrettably.

Marco198 was supposed to visit for Easter long-weekend this year, but he never materialized at the Tampa airport where we waited with a half bottle of Canadian Pinot Gris chilling at home, in his honor. We found out when we returned to our condo, via an e-mail from Marco198's father, Duane, that his son wasn't able to make the flight. Duane explained that

Marco198 had a high school mid-term to study for and, more import-antly, he disapproved of his eighteen year old son traveling to a strange city to meet people he didn't know the first thing about. Brenda and I had a great laugh about the whole situation. We thought it was fitting and funny that when we met in 1999, the person who'd introduced us had been a twelve year-old boy. After we closed the e-mail, Brenda and I enjoyed a steak dinner, followed by a lengthy boning session and an excellent half bottle of white wine.

When we left the restaurant on our first date, Brenda and I walked to her car where I planned to kiss her good night and, since I'd taken the bus to the theatre, ask for a ride home. When we reached her Elantra, we discovered a black Ford Expedition parked over the line, no more than sixteen inches from her passenger side door.

"Would you look at that," I said. "How the heck does this asshole expect someone to get through here?"

"Ridiculous," Brenda said. "And check out that silly license plate." I stepped around the Expedition. In the front of the truck was a gold license plate frame with the personalized plate "C-Dog."

"C-Dog," I said. "Fucking McGriff."

"What are you talking about?" Brenda asked.

"C-Dog," I replied. "His nickname is Crime Dog. That pompous fucker." With her keys in her hand, Brenda came over to the front of the truck and shook her head. She took a quick look over her shoulder and then projected a mouthful of saliva onto the windshield.

"Let's get out of here," she said. "Quick, I'll drive you home." Brenda got into her car and backed out so I would be able to open the passenger door. I rubbed the side of her car, pretending I'd discovered a dent where McGriff had carelessly banged her Elantra with his obscene, SUV door.

"Hold on a second," I said. "Keep the engine running."

I walked back over to McGriff's Expedition and I smoothed out the sleeve of my sport coat. I stood with my back to the driver side door and made sure no one was in the area. After four swift blows, I had my elbow through the driver side window and there was shattered glass all over McGriff's front seat. I sprinted toward Brenda's idling Elantra and jumped in.

"Hurry," I said. "Step on it. McGriff saw me, he's coming." This wasn't true, I hadn't seen McGriff, but it felt like an exciting thing to do. Brenda put her foot firmly on the gas pedal and we peeled out of the parking lot onto John F. Kennedy Blvd.

"That was incredible," she said as she ran a yellow traffic light. *"Eso fue increíble."*

"Can you see him coming?" I asked, pretending I feared McGriff trailing us in a high-speed chase.

"No," Brenda said. "We must have lost him."

"Great," I said.

"Listen," Brenda said. "What do you say we head back to my place for a glass of wine. No funny business, just another glass of wine."

"No funny business," I said. "A glass of wine and some friendly boning."

Brenda laughed approvingly. She flicked on her turning signal and merged onto Route 275. There was a smile on her face as she changed lanes, stepped on the accelerator and took one last glance in the rearview mirror for McGriff.

Johnson's Johnson

This all starts with a baseball card. That one totem, the baseball version of the bar mitzvah, the object after which a ball player can be called major league. Johnson's baseball card had a flaw. Flaw is a good word for it. Mistake is too harsh and, given the circumstances, perhaps a touch too cruel.

Johnson was a good kid. An unspectacular boy growing up in unspectacular Peru, Illinois. Terry Johnson had one gift, the kind of gift that unspectacular boys across America dream about to lift them out of their unspectacularness. He played baseball. He was The Can't Miss Kid of North-Central Illinois. This is what the local paper called him. An all-round player who could field and hit, possessed of a golden arm, an accurate throw, lightning quick reflexes, a heavy bat. Size 12 feet. For whatever reason, everyone knew this about him as well.

The spectacular kids in this part of Illinois all go on to play football or basketball. The unspectacular ones play baseball. And Johnson was the best of the lot.

He got drafted out of high school by the Chicago Cubs. In Peru, they celebrated with a Terry Johnson Day, consisting of parade, a fried chicken dinner in the middle of town, speeches. Terry received a key to the city from the mayor. Townspeople figured his future was assured. That he got drafted by the home team was simply God working His wonders.

Terry reported for Rookie League duty with the team in Mesa, which he found hot, but at least the heat was dry. He settled in at third base, drew the attention of the Cubs brass with his stellar defensive play and before the season was out was up in Boise. In the off-season, he returned to Arizona to play winter ball and concentrate on his hitting and in the spring was asked to report to the AA team in Jackson, TN. And then he broke his wrist fielding a routine bunt and lost a season.

Fortunately for him, he was in the Chicago Cubs system. As his coach in Jackson said: "Son, the Cubs have perfected the art of finding new ways to suck. You're a good third baseman. You'll be in the show soon enough."

He rehabbed in Chicago, attended games at Wrigley, breathed in the air of major league baseball with visions of glory dancing in his head. The team put him up in a luxury hotel just north of the Loop. He delighted in being able to order up burgers through room service. His dad came up to Chicago and Johnson gave him a tour of the innards of Wrigley: the clubhouse, the weight room, the dugout. His dad was impressed. And proud. Johnson was the happiest son in the world.

He returned to Jackson and finished the season strongly. The next winter, he was told he would be attending the Cubs' spring training camp in Mesa. He signed a new contract. He bought his dad a lightning blue Dodge Durango with his signing bonus.

The first two days of camp went by like a blur. The condiments on the buffet table were proof of the elevated station of his life. "Just wait until the regulars get here," a training room guy said. "You're going to see some sweet, sweet food on that table. You don't serve a millionaire a peanut butter sandwich."

The following week, with camp in full swing, Terry Johnson had four photographs taken by six different baseball card companies. He was thrilled. He felt, finally, as if he belonged. He called his father and they marvelled at the path Johnson's life had taken and how far he had come. He was still only 21. He had just earned the right to drink in every state.

He did not notice the flaw in the card issued by the Topps Company.

Johnson was cut from camp and assigned to AAA Des Moines. One step from the bigs, close enough to home that his parents could take in his play, he could taste his coming achievement. Des Moines was like Peru but a lot bigger and with more Mexicans. And then the Cubs pulled off one of those blockbuster trades that make headlines for weeks and burn up phone lines and cause a lot of shouting and consternation in the media and out of it they found themselves with one of the games' best third basemen. Johnson read the news and called up his agent. "What does it mean for me?" he asked.

"It's not good, I'm going to be honest," his agent said.

"I want to play for the Cubs. They're my team," Johnson said.

"I know. But I'm going to be honest, kid, this isn't good for you."

"I'm at three on the depth chart now."

"At least," the agent said.

Johnson spent the next two weeks tearing up AAA. He hit north of .500, with highlight reel plays in the field. His play made him impossible to ignore. He was named the league's player of the week. Pete Gammons mentioned his name on ESPN. A week later, in early July, the Cubs lost two players on the same play, a clumsy play worthy of every sports blooper show in the world if only the thing hadn't hurt the two players so much. An out-of-reach game. The Cubs in the field playing their second string. And the back-up third baseman goes running after a pop up in foul territory, he goes after it hard, perhaps too hard, perhaps because he knows he needs to live the cliché and really put in 110% every time he gets on the field, what with the blockbuster trade and all, and he leaps for the ball, barrelling into the dugout, his cleats carving a map into the chest of the all-star third baseman. The third basemen goes head first into the concrete floor of the dugout. Mayhem ensues. And Johnson gets called up just before the Cubs are set to embark on a road trip. With stops in Montreal, New York, and Philadelphia.

And this is when the flaw in the card is discovered. A collector in Chicago examines Johnson's Topps card. Johnson is leaning forward, his glove at the ready, awaiting the next screamer into the hot corner. He looks like a cheetah stalking antelope. He is serious, professional. Expectant. In his eyes, the confidence and ambition of someone who truly believes he is a major leaguer. There is a hole in his pants. In the crotch. And out of this hole, something. Let's just say this: Johnson did not wear his jock strap that morning. They were only taking pictures after all. He would not need it. At least that was his thinking. It's a rookie mistake. No one told him. And while that something peering out of the hole is not all that clear, there can be no doubt as to what it is. The shape is too familiar.

This collector posts the news on his website. Everyone picks it up. A small story at the end of SportCenter. Letterman jokes about it. An indie band in Milwaukee renames themselves Johnson's Johnson. Immediately, they book themselves on a month long tour of the upper Midwest. The press they receive is like an avalanche. Their music doesn't improve because of this. But they are bigger as a result of the change. It is, simply, a message about the power of branding.

Terry's father calls him and tells him not to worry about it. This is just one of those things; it will blow over. He's a ball player, not a model. Johnson hears no end to the ribbing once he enters the Wrigley Field clubhouse. The pitching coach calls him Johnson Squared, which goes above Johnson's head and keeps sailing, all the way to Waveland Avenue. Johnson gets his locker. And then is told to pack up. He's given coordinates and told to report back at Wrigley Field in four hours for the trip to the airport. His papers are checked. He's given the standard rookie orientation kit. The manager comes over and sits down next to him, welcomes him to the big leagues, and tells him he's here for as long as he deserves it, that his play will determine when and if he's sent down, not the players on the injury list. Only *he* can lose his spot on the roster. The manager tells him he's studied the tapes and considers him an upgrade in the field. "Let's get to work, son," he says, patting his back.

Johnson returns to his hotel room and packs. He's never left the US before and the thought inspires a bit of panic in him. He's heard about the women in Montreal, the nightlife, the tedium of playing at Olympic Stadium in front of six people. He's finally in the big leagues and he's not even playing the US. He's playing in a stadium the players have called a toilet bowl. His family will watch the game on TV.

The flight is game of poker. Johnson is told before the first hand that he should never win, it's a right a rookie has yet to earn and so when he draws a flush, he puts his cards down and folds. In this way, the flight costs him two hundred dollars; the cavalier way in which big leaguers play with money is something that feels wrong to the son of a tractor salesman from Peru, Illinois.

The team checks into their hotel and most of the players nap. Johnson can't. He stares out the window of the hotel, marvels at the foreign languages he hears on the television, searches for ESPN on the TV and gives up, stretches and stretches some more. He showers. He calls his father. "I'm nervous," he admits. "I can't believe this is happening."

"It's all you've ever wanted," his father says.

"I'm going to puke," Johnson says.

And he does.

Later, a bus takes the team to the stadium, a structure that hovers before them like a concrete spaceship. The bus enters the bowels of the thing and the team enters the locker room to suit up and take batting practice. Johnson walks out onto the field and is... underwhelmed. The orange roof. The concrete arches. The yellow and blue seats. "Told ya, it's like a toilet bowl," says the starting second baseman, a fleet-footed black kid from Miami just two years Johnson's senior who won over two thousand dollars on the flight over.

Johnson checks the line up card; he's hitting sixth. In the first inning, the Cubs load the bases on three walks. The clean-up hitter strikes out. Johnson saunters over to the on deck circle. There are perhaps a thousand people in the stands. He can hear a man selling popcorn in two languages. Everything here is in two languages and it is disconcerting. Johnson has heard a lot of Spanish in his baseball life but French is something else. In the fifth spot, the centre fielder, a bruising Dominican, promptly strafes one into left field scoring two. Johnson steps up to the plate. He takes in the scene and hears a mother tell her daughter she can't have any ice cream. "I brought carrots for you," the mother says. Johnson feels ripped-off somehow. He's played in front of more people in the minors. He gets angry. "Is this all there is?" he asks himself. And he strikes out on three pitches.

In the fourth inning, he throws a routine grounder into the Expos' dugout.

In the fifth, he notices a chesty blond in a tight white t-shirt holding up a sign in the empty seats down the right field foul line. It says: Show us your johnson Johnson!

In the eighth, he drops a pop fly.

Later, at a strip club, watching a stage with fifty naked women, one hundred breasts, undulating to the stoner horniness of Snoop Dogg, Johnson downs a beer and yells "Fuck!" No one hears him. The vast fields of nudity, the endlesness of it, the Amazonian expanse of Amazons, it must be noted, does nothing to his johnson.

He is benched the second game.

In the third game, Johnson rips one into the left field corner. The first base coach waves him on. Johnson turns first and feels a pop. He hears it. A pop. It is a bat not quite connecting on a fastball. It is the loudest sound in the stadium. Before he has even hit the ground, he knows it is broken. He tries to crawl to first base. He has the presence of mind to try. But the first baseman tags him out. "Sorry, man," he says.

At the hospital, Johnson is attended to by a nurse that he thinks should come with wings. She holds his hand as the doctor sets his ankle and strokes his hair as the reality of a shattered ankle hits Johnson with the force of twister. He sees the end of his career. She says "no."

"I'm finished," he says. "I'm done," he says. "I'm going to go home and sell tractors," he says.

"Don't give up," she says.

Johnson returns to Chicago. His despair flooded by a tsunami of determination. He heard what she said. She helped him and he feels he owes her something. He hits rehab with gusto.

Her name was Linda. The nurse. The nurse's name was Linda. Johnson was so pathetic, she gave him her e-mail address. And now Johnson decides to use it. And they start flirting on line. And Johnson learns first hand how dirty a word can be. And what kind of turn on a turn of phrase can be. And the intimacy that can develop between two people miles apart just because one of them loads each and every word with innuendo. With meaning. And it isn't him.

The ankle is going nowhere. Johnson was right to feel so pessimistic the night of the break. Two months later, and Johnson's ankle is nothing. It is not doing its job. The ankle has lost mobility. The team doctor says this is going to take at least six months. Johnson asks Linda to come down to Chicago. He sends her airplane tickets. She's never been to Chicago.

After she leaves two days later, she still can't say she has seen anything in the city. Johnson is pretty sure he is going to marry her.

At the airport, he tells her he loves her. "You're just saying that," she says.

It's true, he says.

"I love you, too," she says. And with that she turns and goes through security and is gone.

Standing there, watching her leave, he takes out his cellphone and calls his father. "I met the girl I'm going to marry," he says.

"The nurse?" the father asks.

"I'm in love."

"I'm happy for you, son."

"She's it."

"That's good, son," the father says. "If she's a nurse, she's a good person."

"She is."

"And the ankle?"

And with this question, Johnson breaks down.

When Johnson was three years old, he told his first joke: He danced around the kitchen singing "Poo poo Peru." He repeated this like a koan until his mother banished him to his room. For some reason, Johnson hears this during rehab. When the old black man is stretching his ankle in ways it does not want to go, he hears "Poo poo Peru."

Rehab goes nowhere. It leads to Peru. To Johnson on his parents' couch, red and orange, twenty years old, threadbare, a couch that has witnessed things Johnson would be ashamed to admit to his mother. Out for a walk, exploring childhood haunts, Johnson comes across the old ball field. Above it, Old Glory flutters against an ocean blue sky. This is America, a postcard from another era, and it is where Johnson lived out his dreams of youth. He sees the field and he feels young. And he runs toward it. And he realizes he can't. He can't even push himself into a trot. He is incapable of anything more than a spirited walk. He could not run away from a dog.

He returns to his parents' home. He calls Linda. "I have to quit," he says. "I can't do it. I can hardly walk. This isn't going to work."

Linda listens to him and listens to him cry and she feels what he feels and understands the helplessness of being thousands of miles away when the man you love is spitting on his dream, is admitting the end of a life and she knows she wants to be there when he starts his life anew. "I'm coming," she says. "I'm coming to Peru."

Johnson's Johnson releases an album that all the critics notice. Relegated to a college favorite on campuses all across the Upper Midwest, the band is suddenly national. They feel this. They are booked nationally. They play Jimmy Kimmel. In England, the NME, in its usual extravagent self, calls them "The most magnificent American band playing right now." They play New York's Mercury Lounge for four nights. They play Austin City Limits. The album, called *Squibbler,* cements their status in the country's indie rock firmament. On the back, amidst a collage designed by the lead singer's girlfriend, is the Topps card, a sly reference to the origins of the band's name.

With Linda by his side, Johnson announces his retirement to three reporters and family and friends, and a representative from his agents' office, in the gym of his old school in Peru. His agent gets him a meeting with a sports talk station in Chicago. Big Jim McNeil, "The loudest mouth in Chicago" is a fan of Johnson's Johnson. And thinks it would "fit" to have the real Johnson on the show as part of his "Den." Before the interview, Johnson stops by a bar on Rush for a drink. Which becomes three. Which becomes a rumination on the sorry arc of his career, on the anger he feels toward Montreal, on the nature of dreams. On the fickleness of fate. "You sound like a Baptist," the bartender says.

Despite the alcohol, or perhaps because of it, Johnson slays during the interview. Big Jim sees in Johnson a soul mate, a kindred spirit, a Midwestern kid worthy of something more than life has dealt him. Someone broken down but not broken. Johnson starts in a two weeks.

Later that evening, enjoying a steak with Linda, he asks her to marry him. "You've had four beers," she tells him.

"Doesn't matter," he says. "I could be drinking milk. I've wanted to marry you forever. I know it's true. You're for me."

He doesn't have a ring. And so next day he buys one. And he asks her again. This time in front of Wrigley Field. And this time he has a ring for her. And this time she says yes.

They buy a house in Oak Park. Linda finds a job in a hospital in Palatine. Johnson buys a red Mustang. He starts work. And his riff, for whatever reason, becomes Montreal. At least once a show, he let's go with some bile. Helped, no doubt, by his pre-show drink. Big Jim calls Montreal "Johnson's Waterloo." A sample riff: "I had big league dreams. I was a little kid from a little town in Illinois and I played ball and I could have lived the American dream but I got called up to the Majors to play in a two-bit stadium in a foreign city where they don't even speak English and I broke my stupid ankle in front of ten people. I got called up to the majors and I played a minor league team in a minor league town. There was loser written all over this thing. From the start. Loser! I was a major league loser. And that was that. The most big league thing I ever did was go to a strip club and lose two hundred bucks playing poker on a god damned airplane. I got to eat from the players' buffet at Wrigley. And now I'm on a stupid radio show. I'm such a loser!"

The audience loves it. During his riffs, which can come on at any time, Big Jim can be heard guffawing. You can almost see his belly hopping up and down. His big belly. In Chicago, a name like Big Jim is almost redundant.

Johnson is an angry man. There is no doubt about it. And his anger is somehow paying off. The audience likes it. He represents everyone who ever thought they could somehow make it if only things weren't so stacked against them. He drinks. When Linda announces her pregnancy, Johnson is already pickled. He's had three bourbons and two beers after work. His usual. He slobbers kisses on her and she recoils. She feels alone in this city. She is worried by his drinking. She feels helpless to do anything about it.

That weekend, in Peru, Johnson and Linda announce the pregnancy. Johnson's parents cry tears of joy. Johnson's father pulls out stale cigars. Johnson's mother takes Linda aside and takes her to Johnson's old bedroom. The shelf is festooned with his baseball trophies. They glimmer. Johnson's mother still dusts in here. She hands Linda a pair of baby shoes and a blanket. "These were Terry's," she says.

"Mom, I'm worried about him," Linda says. "He's drinking too much."

Linda contacts the major league players' union and they recommend a counsellor not far from their house. Johnson is incensed. The insinuation is, to him, nothing more than a show of a deep and abiding disloyalty. He does not think he needs help. He storms out.

On the next show: "I hate Montreal. I hate that place. That place has good strippers and that's it. The strippers are awesome. You should see them! Fifty on stage at once. Naked! That's one hundred headlights shaking in your face! Otherwise, nothing good has ever come out of that place. I hate it. They eat weird food there. They put gravy on their fries with this squeaky cheese. The cheese squeaks. It's like putting a squirrel in your mouth or something. They don't have bourbon in the bars. I kid you not. Nothing good ever came out of that place. I went to Montreal and all I got out of it was a wife!" Big Jim likes that line a lot.

Linda doesn't. "You need help," she tells him.

"I don't want to hear it."

"I'm not bringing a child into this kind of house," she says.

"Do what you have to do," he sneers.

And she does. The next day, she's gone by the time he's home from work. He only finds the note the next morning. He calls in sick to work. He drinks until he passes out, on the dining room table. He pisses his pants and he doesn't care. He knows he's hit bottom. He calls the show later that day and delivers a drunken rant that has Jim checking his watch. When Johnson starts screaming, "I love you Big Jim! You're my family!" Big Jim has the good sense to hang up.

The next day, Johnson calls the counsellor.

He puts the house on the market. Linda sends a letter telling him that she has a lawyer and will be writing up divorce papers. She concedes that she gave up early. She doesn't apologize for it, however. She says she's keeping the baby. They can work that out later.

Johnson buys a condo in Wrigleyville. He didn't set out to. It just happened. He buys a loft, big, airy, bright. He's going to be an urban bachelor. From one corner, he can make out the lights of Wrigley Field. He starts to eat a lot of burritos. He joins a gym. The radio show is the number one rated sports talk show in the city. He attains a level of celebrity, a middle class of fame, that feels right to him. He feels he's where he deserves to be.

On this Saturday, he decides to take in a ball game at Wrigley. The sun is warm, the sky hazy with the summer's heat. Baseball weather. He heads out on the twenty minute walk and comes across a garage sale. He peruses the racks, the books on sale, the CDs. He finds a CD by *Johnson's Johnson*. Their first one. On the back, the baseball card. He stares at it, at the hole. The fault. The thing. What would life have been like if he'd just worn his jock strap that morning? Johnson buys it for two dollars. And then he places it on the street and watches as the traffic stomps it until it is nothing but dust.

No Cheering

I'm in the Ballpark in Arlington, several hours before a night game, standing on the track between the dugout and the grass. The track feels pebbly beneath my sneakers. The color of the natural dirt outside the Ballpark is a dusty raw umber. The color of the "dirt" in the ballpark is reddish-orange, like smoked salmon. I step onto the grass, which seems intended to simulate Astroturf. It's bright green and has the bristly spring of indoor-outdoor carpet. Here and there, panels of the grass lift up to reveal hose connections or electrical outlets. The field is as flat as a parking lot.

When you come up the ramp into the stands in a baseball stadium and first see that expanse of green field, it's a gorgeous pastoral vision. Pull away–say, to 5,000 feet in an airliner–and the same park looks like a bit of colored tile in the mosaic of the city. Go up close enough–let's say, stand right on it–and the field might as well be a sheet of plastic. It all depends on perspective.

At the age of 39, with no previous training, I became a professional sportswriter. It was 1998, and in those days, it was pretty easy for people with no experience to do almost anything. You could become a bookstore impresario, a muckraking journalist, or the star of your own web-cam net-cast–all you needed was an Internet connection. If you knew how to hit the Start button, venture capitalists would throw millions at you. They only threw hundreds at me, but it was enough to turn me briefly from a college professor into a baseball columnist. Like Cinderella rising from the ashes, I closed my eyes and was transmuted in an instant from fan to writer, from way outside baseball to–well, to "Outside Baseball," as I called my column: from the kid peering through the window of the candy store to the kid with his nose pressed up against the glass of the candy counter.

The Ballpark is only a few years old, and already the dugout is dilapidated. The bench is newly painted but deeply gouged. Everything is stained, scuffed, gouged by cleats, battered with the impact of bats and balls. This is the major leagues, but the facilities are as ratty as anything at a park-and-rec field.

Ballplayers are not physically reticent. Half carry themselves demurely, but heavily all the same; they punish the turf they walk on. The other half are like large browsing animals. They live to knock things around.

I'm in the Ranger dugout watching batting practice. Two bench players—Roberto Kelly and Luis Alicea—come up out of the tunnel and sit next to me. Kelly carries a glove and Alicea carries a bat. Alicea balances his bat vertically, barrel down, on the dugout floor. Kelly takes the glove and bends it all the way backward, so that the outside of the thumb touches the outside of the little finger. He smacks it several times on his knee. Then he picks up the glove and impales it on the knob of Alicea's bat. Alicea holds the bat steady while Kelly slams the glove on the bat over and over again. They start to giggle.

"New glove?" I ask Alicea. He laughs uncontrollably.

Kelly stops abusing the glove and steps up onto the top step of the dugout. He looks out over the field. Some fans behind the dugout begin to squeal. "Hey, Kelly," they say, "Kelly, can I have your autograph? Can I have your batting gloves? Can you sign your batting gloves and give them to me?" Kelly ignores them.

One shift of regulars finishes batting practice and wanders over to the dugout, sweating in the Texas sun. "Ooooowweeayyahh," says the second baseman, Mark McLemore. "Auugghhieeyyyaawaahhhh!" I wonder if I can quote him on that. McLemore takes cupfuls of water from the cooler and throws them in the general direction of his mouth, swallowing some, drenching his shirt. He throws his cup on the floor and takes another cup and does the same thing. Each player uses two or three cups in this way. Drifts of giant paper snowflakes mound up in the corners of the dugout.

I head back down the tunnel to the clubhouse. Near the clubhouse door, a rookie named Kelly Dransfeldt stands over a wastebasket. With what looks like the jawbone of an ox, he scrapes the handle of his bat. Dransfeldt works away like a paleolithic flintknapper. He looks up at me and bares his teeth in satisfaction. I turn around and head back to the dugout.

The Rangers start to go inside, and the visiting team takes the field for batting practice. I sit in the home dugout as the Rangers pass into the tunnel, and I'm still there after they've all left, sitting like a piece of seaweed left behind after a receding wave. It's always the same with visiting teams; I recognize hardly anyone. The players are young and faceless, dressed in a uniform grey. If I've left my press guide upstairs, I don't have a chance of identifying more than a few veteran players.

The coaches, though, can touch off Proustian flashes of memory. One night I wander around to the third-base side of the batting cage and spot an outsized man signing autographs. The hip pockets of his uniform are full of baseballs. They protrude like warty excrescences on the hindquarters of an ape. Something about the man's shoulders reminds me of the sixth grade. As he turns back toward the field, I realize why: it's Frank Howard, a home-run champion from the late 1960s, a man whose picture covered the yearbooks and magazines I bought when I was ten years old. He plods to the fungo circle and starts to pick baseballs out of the pouches on his rump. Looking like Atlas weary of supporting the world, he pops the balls into center field with his bat.

Another night, the visitors' batting practice breaks up, and the young players skip back to the dugout and down the tunnel. Left behind is a coach carrying a milk crate. He stoops over to pick up every baseball that the hitters have left behind on the infield, the ones they have bunted, beaten into the turf, lined with a clang off the screen that protects the pitcher. He straightens up and looks at me. It's Jim Rice, a 1970s All-Star, a rookie when I started college. He's not much older than I am, but he's old enough to be the father of some of his players. He works out a kink in his back and goes back to gleaning baseballs.

I head up to the press box. The elevator operator smiles at me. A stout, white-haired man, he spends the hours before and after each game crouched on a tiny stool in the press elevator, watching other sports on TV. He always remarks on the sport he's watching, expecting me to have an intimate acquaintance with, and a burning interest in, the University of Cincinnati's pass rush or the Lady Raiders' zone defense. I respond with emphatic phrases like, "How about that?"

The pressbox smells of aftershave. In fact, everything behind the scenes of the ballpark smells of aftershave, except for the visitors' clubhouse, which smells of despair. You walk along the upstairs corridors in a mist of aftershave, into an elevator redolent of aftershave, down into the home clubhouse full of freshly shaven young men splashing aftershave. Even the occasional woman writer seems to wear aftershave.

I sit down, spread out, and settle in to stare out the window. Visiting sluggers pound home runs over the fence. In center field, there's an open area, grassed in to serve as a "batter's eye"—a green space for the white ball to emerge from when the pitcher sends it towards home plate. Some of the batting-practice homers land on this lawn. When one does, kids who have been held back by the guards are allowed to swarm around the ball. From this distance, they look like hosts of antibodies surrounding invader bacteria on a microscope slide. Finally one kid holds the ball up, and the rest retreat to wait for the next one.

After the visitors leave the field, the groundskeepers come out and dismantle the big backstop. The fans who have queued up for autographs disperse in search of cheese fries. The field looks more forlorn than expectant. A couple of players do private rituals of sprints or stretching. A groundskeeper carries a rake aimlessly from one corner of the diamond to the other.

Ballclub public relations officers, like Nature, abhor a vacuum. The empty moments don't last long. Silently (to me, glassed into the sound-proof press box), a crowd of people pours out of the leftfield door and onto the warning track. Leading the way are a pantomime chicken and pantomime cow carrying a banner that reads FLOWER MOUND LITTLE LEAGUE. Flower Mound is a suburb of Fort Worth where people "build." Ask middle-class people in Tarrant County where they live and they reply coyly, "we're building in Flower Mound." They may be "staying" in a starter house for the time being, but soon they will make it to Flower Mound.

A lot of building has gone on in Flower Mound. Cadre after cadre of fourth-graders in baseball uniforms tumble out of the great door and join the parade. The Flower Mounders circle the field and leave by the same door, and still they come. I had not thought death had undone so many. Past home plate they tramp, miniature gaggles of Rangers and Angels and Diamondbacks. It must be the same people who have just left the field coming back on again, an Anglo-American fire drill. So many people cannot all be so blond and so happy.

At last the Flower Mound wave is spent. The kids leave the field. The chicken and cow stay. The cow dons a sandwich board that says EAT MOR CHIKIN. The implication is that cows might be intelligent enough to learn to write, but not intelligent enough to become good spellers.

The chicken does not have a sign that says EET MOR KOW. He catches up to the cow in front of the visitors' dugout. The chicken prances around the cow, making little fluttery chicken charges. An ugly confrontation seems to be brewing. A ballpark security man goes out and appeases the cow and chicken. They make their way lugubriously around the warning track. In front of the home dugout, they start to scuffle again.

Finally the chicken and cow make amends. They get together to preside over a contest. A contestant named Mark is fixing to try to catch a baseball popped into the air from a pitching machine. If he catches the ball, everyone in the park wins a free Coke. Ballpark Cokes are huge buckets of ice, with a mist of Coke over the top, that sell for four dollars. It's no great prize to win one, but at least you save four dollars.

Mark stands near the left-field foul line, waving his glove. The machine is in center field. A baseball pops into the air. Mark weaves drunkenly around. Then he spots the ball and sprints forward decisively. But his decision was not good. He seriously overruns the ball. He watches it fly over his head toward the stands. Mark staggers backward like a man caught square in the chest with a blast from a firehose, stabbing the air with his arms, finally landing flat on his back as the ball drops several yards behind him. No Coke tonight.

I get pretty thirsty before games myself. Unlike the fans, I can fill up my own Coke, without ice, for free. Free snacks, all of them unhealthy and most of them disgusting, are laid on for the press before and during ballgames. The media eat constantly. It's my impression that the casual media, here only on home stands and many (like me) here only for certain games, eat more than the beat-writers who are at every game, and eat lots more than the visiting beat writers whose souls rebel at another plate of steamtable brisket.

The half-hour or so between the cow-and-chicken show and the National Anthem stretches on and on. There's little to see and less to think about. I could read the statistics, the spreadsheets provided by the club that give the batting averages of the players in every conceivable situation, their performances at night, with the bases loaded, against left-handers, in the late innings of close games with the wind blowing in. But I'd rather eat.

I have my rituals. The staple snacks are hotdogs, peanuts, popcorn, and frozen yoghurt. The hotdogs gather a patina as they roll around between stainless-steel cylinders, getting more and more brazen as they turn. I never eat a hotdog. The peanuts are popular, because you can amuse yourself shucking them, but I find them rubbery and oversalted. So I go for the popcorn, eating two tubfuls a kernel at a time, and then head for the frozen yoghurt.

The frozen yoghurt is one of the main conversation starters in the pressbox. We live for the days when they serve chocolate. A vanilla day is, well, a vanilla day. An old scout settles into his chair, spilling papers out of his briefcase, sighing. He was a slugger in the 1960s, a coach in the 70s, a general manager in the 80s, and is now being nice to the people he met on the way up as he descends into the 21st century.

"They got chocolate today," says the next scout over.

The old scout's mask of pain breaks into a half-smile. He bobs up out of his chair and goes over to the yoghurt machine. He pours a big swirly portion of chocolate yoghurt into a clear plastic glass and then squirts chocolate sauce over it. He's seen a lot of things in this game, but few have given him so much pleasure.

I may have been like Cinderella, but I didn't need a fairy godmother to turn me into a sportswriter. All it took was some University of Iowa Ph.D. students in English Lit. 1998 may have been the leading edge of the dot.com wave, but it was the trough of the job market for literature professors. Some Iowa students threw in academic careers to start up an on-line sports magazine. The result was SportsJones.com.

I didn't know any of the Iowa SportsJones people. That was another great thing about the dot.com days–you didn't really have to know anybody. No sherry to sip. No suits to wear, no flesh to be pressed. A couple of e-mail messages and you had a working relationship. A couple more and you were old cronies. Two e-mails with SportsJones, and I was Contributing Editor and senior baseball columnist.

Now I sit here, an accredited sports journalist, a day pass that identifies me as WORKING PRESS pasted to my shirtfront. As a columnist, I don't even have to write about the game that's about to begin; I can write on anything I want, even on the planes flying overhead, towing banners that advertise gentlemen's clubs for sophisticates.

There's a roar from the crowd that penetrates even the thick pressbox glass. Skydivers begin to float into the Ballpark. They land in a tight pattern on the outfield grass. One by one, they gather up their trailing parachutes, like bridesmaids lifting the trains of their dresses. They run off the field towards the visiting dugout. One of them pauses in front of Nomar Garciaparra. He pulls out a pocket notebook and gets Garciaparra's autograph. He sweeps up his skirts and rushes away.

The groundskeepers come out to chalk the baselines. The chalk machine is a thing of beauty, really. It's just a hopper with a hole in the bottom, filled with chalk. It works like a lawn seeder, except that instead of a broadcast, it lays down a neat thick line of chalk. The diamond changes from a scruffy surface into a neatly-drawn box. Everything should be so clean, with such bright lines separating the fair from the foul.

A writer's cellphone rings, playing the Brahms lullaby. He has to search for it in his pile of stats and scoresheets.

I get my third tub of popcorn and start back into the pressbox. As I open the door from the lounge to the pressbox, I stop in my tracks. Everyone in the pressbox is standing silently. Through the tough glass, I can faintly hear the National Anthem. I'm caught in the doorway. Behind me, writers are milling around, laughing, noshing peanuts. Before me, different writers are frozen in the attitudes of patriotism. I don't know what to do. I just stand there. I don't put my hand over my heart, but at least I don't eat any popcorn either.

I don't have a good seat tonight. A lot of scouts were in early, and I had to sit in the third row of seats in the pressbox. Perched on a tall barstool, I'm too high up to get a good angle through the short slit of the pressbox window. I can't see home plate. I can sort of see the pitcher over a TV monitor in the first row, but I lose sight of him during his followthrough. If I scoot to my right, first base comes into view past one of the vertical frames of the window, but I have to get very far up on my tiptoes to see the batter. Most of the time I just watch the game on TV.

Most of the writers are watching TV. Most of them are not watching the game that's being played on the field. They watch playoff hockey. They watch golf. They watch reruns of Olympic events played several hours before in Australia. Their conversation is a farrago of incompatible sporting jargons.

"Hey, the Yankees just put in their nickel D."

"Tiger Woods is going to the rope-a-dope."

"Hey, Colorado's putting on a full-court-press in the Stars' zone, but if they aren't careful Brett Hull's going to hit one over the fence."

All the writers are intensely interested in any event that doesn't happen to be today's baseball game. And with reason. A close baseball game, nowadays, is an aberration. A close, low-scoring game seems as rare as no-hitters were when I was a kid. By the second or third inning, the

Rangers are usually up by seven runs or down by seven runs, and the rest of the evening turns into a showcase for mediocre relief pitchers.

Everything blurs together. You forget who's playing, what place they're in in the standings, who's up at bat. All the clubs seem to wear the same blue uniforms. The Rangers used to wear red, but more and more now they wear blue, the same blue as the Blue Jays. When Toronto gets a couple of men on base, you look down and you think there are six infielders.

You hear it said: people who think baseball is boring don't know the game very well. This might be true; but it's even truer that people who think baseball *isn't* boring don't know it very well at all. People who think baseball isn't boring have not been compelled to watch the Rangers fall behind 10-0 after four innings of a game against the Tigers, in Texas, in late July, on a 90-degree night, after two months without rain. With two out and nobody on, I watch the Rangers' Gabe Kapler step in, step out, step in, take a pitch, step out, do something with his batting gloves, step in, take a pitch, step out, look down to the coach for a sign, step in, step out, grab his helmet, step in, and ground out to third. A. Bartlett Giamatti, literature professor and Commissioner of Baseball, once said that "The game begins in the spring, when everything else begins again, and it blossoms in the summer, filling the afternoons and evenings." The problem is that it fills them entirely too well. It fills four hours of my summer evenings with warm-up pitches and cup adjustments and throws to first base. It underlines like nothing else the futility of human endeavor.

There's no cheering in the pressbox. That's the unwritten rule. It's a cliché, really; the adage is so familiar that Chicago sportswriter Jerome Holtzman made it the title of a book. But the rule is, by and large, observed. Early in my time as a writer, a batter lifts a long fly to right center, dicey work for any centerfielder, and the centerfielder in question is

Roberto Kelly, who is not much younger than I am. When Kelly hauls in the baseball, I rise unconsciously out of my seat to applaud. Immediately, I repress the gesture, because nobody around me is moved in the slightest. That's too bad: it was a major-league catch.

There's no cheering, but scoffing is liberally permitted. As the innings crawl by, Ranger pitcher Aaron Sele allows many long flies to the power alleys. Kelly catches some but can't catch them all. With each new belt to the outfield, the writers breathe more and more audibly in disgust. Soon the whole pressbox is in fact cheering–not for the Rangers, or against them, exactly, but cheering for some Platonic ideal of pitching that is, at this moment, definitely not being represented by Aaron Sele.

As the first innings of a game pass, scouts filter out, to the stands behind home plate, I suppose. Writers and broadcasters filter in to take their places. In the early innings, a gaunt, bald old man comes in and sits to my right. He has a scoresheet, and he starts to keep score. He fidgets and mutters.

I get up for more yoghurt. The old man stops me. Like the Wedding Guest caught by the Ancient Mariner, I make a gesture as if to go. He holds me with his skinny hand.

"I used to play for Connie Mack," he says.

"That's great," I say. I look into my empty yoghurt cup.

"They don't listen to me anymore," he says.

"Who doesn't listen to you?" I say.

"The hitters." He looks into my eyes. "I tell them, choke up, move your front foot in, protect the plate. I told Palmeiro that, you think he listens? He tries to hit the ball out of the park every God damn time." Sure enough, on the TV monitor behind the old man's shoulder, Palmeiro fishes at strike three.

"They don't listen," I say.

"I knew you would understand," he says. "You look like the kind of guy who'd understand. I played on the Senators for Bucky Harris, he knew what to do. Lou Gehrig said I was one of the best young talents he ever played against."

Gehrig has been dead for almost sixty years. I look at the old man, the sagging skin on his frame, an animal held together by fibers of memory. I think of the meals, the drinks, the lovers, the vacations he's had in sixty years, the clothes he's worn, the cars he's driven, the cakes of soap he's lathered into nothingness on his body in sixty years of showers. I think of all the baseball he's watched since Gehrig died, the sourness, the joy.

"Did you know Ossie Bluege?" I say, picking a name out of my limited knowledge of the old Senators. Of course he did. "Ossie Bluege and I were married on the same day, in West Virginia. But how would you know about him? Now most people would barely remember Ossie Bluege." He squints at me. It's clear that he cannot place my age. I could be twenty or eighty; it could be 1999 or 1939. He starts a long story about Bluege, about baseball, about women. Behind him, behind the plate glass of the pressbox window, tiny men in white and grey move silently around the field, chasing the ball.

I come back to the box with my yoghurt. Some writers are gathered around a TV monitor. They are watching *Wheel of Fortune*. The puzzle shows R_T_ CR_C_ _RS.

"Can I buy an 'O'?" asks the contestant.

"It's RITZ CRACKERS," says a writer. "RITZ CRACKERS, can you imagine it? 'Can I buy an "O"'? Jesus Christ on crutches."

I sit back down and try to watch some of the game. I crane my neck so I can see Hideo Nomo go into his windup. He looks like a shotputter on the bottom of the sea. Sounds of the dwindling, restless crowd come piped into the pressbox over the audio system. Since the glass is virtually soundproof, the noise of the crowd is captured for us by a microphone in the stands. I wonder if it's live. The crowd is making generic noises that seem unconnected to the game.

The next thing I know, the pressbox is filled with sneezes. The crowd mike must be next to a man who is having a sneezing fit. It is unpleasant to listen to someone sneeze continuously for a minute and a half, but in a way it's reassuring. They wouldn't put a ninety-second sneezing fit on a tape of Standard Crowd Noises, so the audio feed must be live. The sneezing dies away, and the background chant of a vendor rises again: "Beer! Beer here! Co' beer!"

A kid comes into the pressbox with an armful of baseball bats. "You want a bat?" he asks me. I think, why not. I put the bat carefully under my desk. Most writers take a bat. Some sit it on the desk, some clutch it between their legs. One guy stands up in the aisle and practices a batting stance. Another pounds the bat into his free palm, making smacking noises.

In the middle innings, an immensely fat radio personality comes into the pressbox. He sits in the front row, next to the only woman in the box. I don't know what her job is, exactly; she seems to do nothing except pick up the phone after each pitching change and tell some anonymous expectant listener that the change has been made. The fat man takes off his headset, lays down his microphone, divests himself of his tape recorder and various other peripherals.

"What kind of yoghurt they got?" he asks the woman.

"Chocolate," she says.

"I'm'a get some chocolate," he says. "Later I'll get some chocolate. You got some of them peanuts?" He takes a mittful of peanuts from her cup. "Had lasagne for dinner," he mentions, not so much to the woman as to the air. "Olive Garden. They bring out the lasagne, it's all you can eat, salad, garlic bread. Three kinds of lasagne. I had the spinach lasagne, it's better for you, vitamins. They have this vegetarian too, it's kind of got eggplant. Like eggplant parmigiani. I don't like the cheese. I don't like the desserts. Salad's good. You going to eat them peanuts?"

The woman surrenders her peanuts. He eats them thoughtfully.

"Who started?" he asks, glancing at the scoreboard.

"Sele," she says.

"Got his head beat in. No intestinal fortitude," he says.

"Huh?" she says.

"No guts. Sele. He's a quitter. It's a fact, he's a quitter, no guts." She nods and taps her pencil.

"Once I was in the clubhouse and Reggie Jackson was there," he says. "Reggie Jackson was there, and all these guys, it was the A's in town, the old stadium, and these guys were all around, like writers and players. And Reggie Jackson farted."

He gets no reaction. He starts to laugh at his own story.

"Reggie Jackson," he says. "And all these guys around, and Reggie Jackson farted."

I keep waiting for a foul ball to hit the glass, but in two years, it never happens. The pressbox has a peculiar design. Not only is the front window onto the field glass, but the roof is glass as well. The blinds that screen the place from the worst of the day-game sun roll not just up and down the front but back and forth across the top as well. It's the first place I've worked in that literally has a glass ceiling.

The glass is tempered, I assume. It repels drink cups and hotdogs and the occasional cooler that falls from the upper deck. But I have a residual nervousness about how the glass would hold up to something more powerful, like, say, a foul ball lined straight back, or a human body dropping straight down. But I sit though game after game and never have the chance to find out. Balls hit below and above us, to the right and the left. They fly into the open windows of the radio booth next door. But they never hit the pressbox.

I walk back to use the bathroom. Someone comes the other way. He looks very familiar. He smiles and nods; I nod back. I am sure I know him from around town. Maybe he shops at my supermarket. I look back; he's turned to talk to somebody. Then I realize who he is; he's Jim Palmer, the ex-pitcher and ex-underwear-model. I didn't recognize him fully dressed.

By the seventh inning, the score is something like 14-1. The visitors (maybe they're the Kansas City Royals? I can't remember) have replaced their whole lineup with guys who are even more obscure than the starters. I wonder if anyone could possibly care what happens next. I cling to the idea that this evening, this ghastly ball game that seems to me the very definition of *ennui,* is for some ten-year-old kid in Missouri the apogee of his summer, the one evening when his heroes seemed invincible, when the planets aligned and there was joy in Mudville. Is there, *is* there balm in Gilead? I stare up and out into the Texas night and pray that there is.

In Arlington, at the seventh-inning stretch, they play a tape of "Take Me Out to the Ballgame," or at least a few bars of it. In mid-tune, the tape suddenly swings into the "Cotton-Eyed Joe." This is a moment that strikes fear into my Yankee heart. I sit transfixed, dark-bearded, Slavic-looking, while thousands of clean blond people rise up and start stomping and clapping. Just when all seemed blandly suburban, the crowd becomes a primal white mob, stirred up by the unconscious anthem of their race.

"Seattle and Oakland are playing a four-game series next weekend," says a scout. "A four-game series. Good God. I'd fly a hundred thousand miles to see a four-game series." He's seeing one here, or the bitter dregs of one. As he shakes his head over the prospect of a better one somewhere else, I catch sight of that little thread of hope, a link to childhood—the vision of a summer weekend free from school and camp, and baseball on the radio every blessed day.

On the TV monitor I can see the batter taking his stance. Behind him, a revolving notice board on the wall displays a different ad every few moments. Right now it's an ad for Viagra. The batter strikes out.

The game ends in a flurry of indifference. The visiting catcher, a second-string rookie, races out to shake his pitcher's hand. The pitcher is trudging away and has to be tapped on the shoulder to remind him that congratulations are in order. The writers head in a flock to the elevator. I let the first wave pass and follow a bit later; the managers never appear for about 15 minutes anyway, the players never for 20 or 25. Some of them never appear at all.

The down elevator stops at the luxury-box level. A blonde woman in a fawn-colored suit, tanned, slim, of a heart-arresting loveliness, steps in, carrying an oversized bunch of gladioli. The elevator man introduces her to me. She's the wife of a Rangers' infielder. I shake her hand; I feel as if I should bow over it. We get off the elevator in the basement. She glides to the clubhouse, holding her flowers aloft. She disappears into the recesses where I cannot follow.

I go to the interview room. Writers sit heavily on hard chairs waiting for Rangers' manager Johnny Oates to show up. He strides in, his jaw clenched, his eyes daring anyone to ask a question. No one does ask a question; writers rarely do. They simply make standardized noises that evoke quotes.

The fat radio guy goes first. "Talk about the third inning," he says, the inning of booted grounders and line drives to the wall that chased Aaron Sele from the pitcher's box.

"We didn't have our rhythm going," says Oates.

"Talk about Alicea," prompts another writer. Alicea, the third baseman tonight, made two errors in the third inning.

"I know we can throw the ball better than that," says Oates. His "we" intrigues me. It's akin to the editorial we, the royal we, the doctor's "how are we this morning"; but it's not identical. "I know we can throw better than that": in fact, I know Oates can throw better than that; he was a strong major-league catcher in his day and still pitches a mean batting practice. But Oates actually means that he knows that Alicea can throw the ball better than that. Yet something in his tone indicates that he is by no means assured that Alicea can throw the ball any better than that. He may mean: "If we, or at least one of us named Alicea, cannot throw the ball better than that, then we, or at least Alicea, will be farmed out to Oklahoma City next week."

The writers run out of things that they would like Oates to talk about. He leaves, and the writers shuffle out to the Rangers' clubhouse. Like trial attorneys, sportswriters never ask questions they don't already know the answers to. Sele, the losing pitcher, stands by his locker half-undressed and submits to questioning. No, he did not have his good curve ball tonight. Yes, he found it difficult to get his rhythm. No, he is not discouraged. It's a long season. You have to give these Angels, or these Devil Rays, or whoever, some credit; they're a good-hitting ball club and you can't make mistakes when you pitch to them. Yes, he's looking forward to the Baltimore series. As if he could avoid it. Yes, yes, yes, yes, no.

I look around the clubhouse. Not many players are in evidence. One of the few who come out to dress at their lockers is a relief pitcher about my own age named Mike Morgan. He has been pitching major-league ball since the 1970s, and will pitch for years to come, even helping Arizona win the 2001 World Series. Tonight, he has merely eaten up a few undistinguished innings, given up a few meaningless runs. His body is shapeless and grey. Most of the other players drape themselves with towels and slip quickly into their pants; Morgan wallows unconcerned in his own nakedness.

I wish I could talk to him, but it seems unthinkable; the writers give him a wide berth. It's not that he pitched badly, though he did. It's that no-one cares how he pitches, good bad or indifferent, because he never appears at the crucial moment of any game. His knowledge of baseball, his desire to keep pitching as he heads 40 and turns into the homestretch of his life, his pathos: whatever it all amounts to, it stays locked in his grey body and greyer head.

The writers skip away to ask a 24-year-old to talk about his first big league home run. He says it felt good. I look around the clubhouse as the players get dressed. They change from kids in baseball suits to men in polo shirts; but they looked more like men in the baseball outfits: sharper, more professional. In their grown-up clothes they shrink back into kids again, shy, tentative, in mismatched slacks, in need of their moms. One by one the players turn back into post-adolescents–all but Mike Morgan, naked in his reverie.

An aging actor once told me that it was impossible to play King Lear. You could not understand the role until you were very, very old, but when you got old enough to understand it, you were too old to play it anymore. Baseball is like that. It is wasted on the young people who are the only ones with the energy to play it. There's no sense talking to these people. I would go back upstairs and talk to the Ancient Senator, but he has long since gone off to a fitful sleep.

I step onto the elevator to head up to the street level. The elevator guy is watching the day's highlights on ESPN-something. Somebody's knocked somebody out, and somebody else has won in straight sets. I get out at the ground floor and walk toward the turnstiles. As I leave the gates I peel off my press pass and stick it on to the back of my scorecard. "See you tomorrow," says the guard at the gate.

Then, one day, there was no tomorrow. Early in 2001, the party was over. Dot.com cash-flow became "irregular," the publisher said. SportsJones folded. My press pass turned into Swiss cheese, my spiral pad into a rind of rotten pumpkin. One day I was sitting in the middle of 75 Japanese writers cheering–or rather, not cheering–for Ichiro Suzuki, and the next minute I was sitting at home watching SportsCenter like everybody else. The thing about being Cinderella, though, is that you have been to the ball. Even if all you have to look forward to is sweeping and stepsisters, that one night was enough. And even if the ball was mostly sitting around waiting for princes to come, doodling on your dance-card and eating chocolate frozen yoghurt, it's something to tell your grandchildren about.

Pastime Kit

... we got to the ball park,
it was already dark out
maybe four in the morning
there were millions of fans
and the guy who was with me
on the two-seated bicycle
swore on his mother
that he had a plan.
He had a Kit of some kind
that if inserted rightly
would scramble the minds
of the innocent young
"And make them ours" he said.
"And make them ours" he said.
"And make them ours" he said.
"And make them mine."

He showed me the Kit,
a mass of tightly wound tape-worms,
the guy from my bike
described how the things worked:
"You find a curious kid
and you stuff it up there.
And there's no need to fear getting caught
because kids don't remember.
And there's no need to fear getting caught
because kids don't remember
if it's Melville
or if it's Whitman
or if it's Hawthorne...."

Dear Baseball

I am not a numerologist. "Holy baseball,
Batman, that's nine divine syllables" (says Robin
Ventura). Eight's enough: I'm not a numerologist.
But you're all about *the numbers,* ain't ye!

The cosmos of Pythagoras; your patron,
St. Augustine of Hippo ("Numbers are the
Universal language"), spent 370 A.D.
In Carthaginian cheap seats, cussin' out

The umpire—I mean, Empire (i.e. Roman).
Roman mythology by-the-by speaks of nine Furies:
Geena Davis, Madonna, Rosie O'Donnell, etc.,

None of whom possess a fast ball comparable
To Great Jove "hurling thunderbolts from his mound"
(I mean, "Mount" i.e. incomparable Olympus).

To the Big Leagues in Crisis

I propose the ominous insinuation of political
Intrigue, international in scope; during
The seventh-inning stretch have "Take Me Out
To the Ball Game" accompanied by a zither.

In exasperated reaction to the travesty of 2002's
"Midsummer Classic," I propose it be a
Friendly in which all-stars play transvested in tutu-unis
Against Sayles's slow-pitch *Brooklyn Bimbos.*

And I propose in "The Best Interest of Baseball"
That on the 10th of May every summer every copy
Of every Kevin Costner baseball flick be burned
En masse in expurgatory glee at Cooperstown.

But, to you, the Sport I love, if nothing else, heed
These two words of wisdom: XFL Cheerleaders.

Chironomy (Like "Balk," Nobody *Really* Knows What It Means)

The signing of signs over nine three-out innings over 182 games, plus Spring & post-season;
from bench-coach to base-coach, from
base-coach to catcher, from catcher to pitcher
—a pitch, at last, a fast-ball—Chironomy,
which, in the great *oratorio* we call Baseball
(how lofty a metaphor! a lofty lob; it's up
& down, it's fathers & sons, the orchestra's
sad, sadder song), sends Tullius Cicero (No. 25),
who emphasized gesture, a bird, to the minors
in a minor key, down to single-A Arpinam
to DH for *De Oratore Dodgers* of the Roman League.
He who manages his hands manages the game;
Scritch-scratch your balls into the Hall of Fame.

Baseball Leaves *Montréal*

Even with early frost or freak September
snows, the habitués of *centre-ville* say
the game's grown too hot
for the *très* chic gone lean
on skis, too heavy for scanty
support and a lack of batons.

We broke them in the big icing
that bowed trees, then pursued citizens
to the cellars where we all searched for something
sturdy, in nicked oak, signed by *le Grand Orange.*

Something with enough clout–*eh?*–
to crack crystalline coats along St. Catherine's,
ice sheets over our own windshields, doorknobs,
or a glaze on *le métro's* rails. No want
of wielders, *frappeurs,* the odd *lanceur*
to unfreeze rope.

Not for Montrealers baseball's summer
stink and salt stains, ruddy fans
dripping into seats while those latecomers,
the English-speakers and Yanks,
shout, punch mitts, fire the air.

Mais non, up here, heat seems a necessity
in measured doses, a force held at arm's

length and sought only after a slow
thaw, like rubbing frostbite with ice.

In this province, maybe, we've gotten used
to down, a useful layer, and don't
fully warm to any other losing cause
except that old one we won't forget.

To hold baseball, we can only hope for creeping
cold around the Big O, river slush, and expansion
of frigid water, then a long glaciation, quickening
our pulses but not enough to burn.

Pedro: The Fall 2003

When Pedro pitches, he lances the great fester
of red roar, flattens the edges of puff, ignores
the odd beer-bottle arc, paper meteorites.
His shot's nothing like a mere prick, but
A hard scrape to bare bone.

In home whites, he balls them all together:
tendon and thew, vessel and sac.
He faces each man, soft-mouthed at the set,
thinking stigmata, sliders, a scalpel curve,
then rolls his eyes heavenward,
waiting to eye the sign, blind with light.

Here's no challenge to patient
practice, only a steady coil to center,
where, in a hollow above the hand's heel,
he sweats, kneads skin, and aims,
intent–before, after, perhaps just this once–
to cut a perfect body by chance.

Who Needs Your Stinking Pennant?

No one ever seems to mention the first Montreal Expos pennant race. Allow me to redress that situation.

1973 was a freak year in the National League East, with five out of six teams hovering around the .500 mark all season. The Expos, heretofore known to non-believers mostly for their embarrassing beanie-style caps, suddenly found themselves, without having actually improved much, in the thick of the hunt. Players like Pepe Frias, John Boccabella and Bob "Scrap Iron" Stinson, men had seemed as much comedians as ballplayers, now had a chance to alter the course of history.

Well, the Expos didn't win that year. Of course they didn't. They finished fourth, four games below .500, three and a half games behind Tom Seaver's Mets. To come so close but be denied was iron-clad proof, to my ten year-old self, that the universe was an uncaring place, a moral void where any notion of justice and fairness existed only in order to be mocked and flouted. One magical mid-September morning, though, the standings in the paper told another tale entirely. They read in part like this:

NL EAST

Team	W	L	GB
Montreal	77	74	-
St. Louis	77	74	-

This epochal document, clipped from the Edmonton Journal, was on my bedroom wall all that winter. I would stare at it in a trance as my older brother, a worldly 13, endlessly played Deep Purple's *Machine Head* and Led Zeppelin's *Houses of The Holy*. To this day I cannot hear either of those fine works (the Zeppelin album gets the nod for including "Over The Hills and Far Away") without being briefly seized by the memory and force of those printed figures, especially the chilling "−" indicating that on that one shining morning no one stood higher than my Expos. Thirty-four years later that clipping is still somewhere in my possession.

"Boo frigging hoo," you may well be thinking. "To quote Wittgenstein's friend, 'Get a life, Ludwig.'" And I can understand that. To everyone but a New York Yankees fan, after all, following a team basically means getting an annual lesson in life's essential imperfectability. In the cases of the sad-sack teams, one might go further and invoke the Orwellian metaphor of a boot stomping on a human face forever. Paradoxically, of course, the position of the one being stomped upon is a place that can grow comfy, even reassuring; several Red Sox fans of my acquaintance have described the strange sense of disorientation and hollowness they experienced on waking up the morning after the Curse was lifted. Even a loser's identity is an identity, and to change yours overnight can't be easy.

I will argue, though, that the case of the Expos and their benighted fans is a special one. I'm not sure even Montrealers, let alone Americans, can appreciate what the early Expos meant to kids like me across the Canadian hinterland. Our sense of identification, the sheer desperate need we projected onto these athletes–men who, let's face it, probably viewed playing in Canada as an inconvenience, and longed to be traded to Los Angeles–was so intense that it could at times be literally painful. Once, along with two friends and safely beyond earshot of unsympathetic adults, I openly wept front of the basement TV at the ease with which the powerhouse Pittsburgh Pirates crushed the Expos. But it could work the other way too. I recall with perfect clarity a moment in 1972 when Reds manager Sparky Anderson, being interviewed on Expos Baseball by Duke Snider, called Montreal "a team to watch." I got goose bumps. Here was a validation of our devotion, of our young lives, of our very history as a nation. If it seems silly to you that a grown man named Sparky with a huge chaw of tobacco in one cheek could wield that kind of power, well, you just don't understand and you never will.

I should say, to give a complete picture, that something rendered the first Expos pennant race all the more gripping for me. You see, the previous winter Roberto Clemente had died, and he was my hero. What's the connection? Let me explain.

It may seem strange that my hero would have been a non-Expo, a man who, as a member of the dreaded Pirates, appeared to take extra pleasure in beating my team into the turf. (I'll bet if you went to some geek website and checked the numbers, you'd find Clemente had a phenomenally high average against Montreal.) But Clemente, for me, was such an undeniable force—his skills so dazzling, his manner and bearing so noble and imperious, his moral authority so self-evident—that he overrode the matter of team loyalty. I could not imagine him not being my hero. Then, having finished the 1972 season by getting his 3000th career hit in the last game, Clemente organized a shipment of relief materials to be flown from his native Puerto Rico to earthquake-stricken Nicaragua. Insisting on boarding the small plane himself, he perished along with the crew when the plane went down in a Caribbean storm.

I did not know how to process this. I'd had no experience with death, and feared that I would be taken for funny if I cried over a baseball player. So I internalized it all, and emotionally I floundered. Eventually, grasping, I determined by a complicated but perfectly sound system of kid logic that if the Expos won their division the following year—I dared not think as far ahead as the LCS or Lord forbid, the World Series—then, in some way, the world would be fair again. If the Expos came out on top, order and meaning would be restored. Roberto Clemente's incomprehensible death would be redeemed. Everything would be all right again.

Silly of me, you say? Perhaps. And even if the shaky premise were accepted, wouldn't it have made more sense to root for the Pirates? Technically, yes. But come on. I was ten. And anyway, I've said how that pennant race turned out. The winter of '73-'74 was rough, Purple and Zeppelin notwithstanding.

Naturally that kind of intensity can't be sustained through the trials, bruises and occasional joys of post-childhood life. And that's probably just as well. But it never completely goes away. Let me tell you the saddest story I know.

In 2004 I was a Montreal resident of some six years' standing, having moved there with my wife out of a sense of adventure but also–I'm not sure I ever told my wife this part–because of the Expos. For me the whole city was, and is, infused with their presence. Walking past present-day Jarry Park, now a cold venue for tennis, I swear I feel the lingering spirits of Ron Hunt, Bob Bailey, Steve Renko, Ken Singleton, all those noble soldiers of '73–and, yes, I swear I've glimpsed the ghost of Clemente.

And I did indeed go to many Expos games. I was in the stands, along with no more than a few hundred others, when the Padres' Tony Gwynn got his 3000th hit. I was privileged to witness the ascension to greatness of Vladimir Guerrero, and gasped as prodigal son Pedro Martinez, back in town with the Red Sox for an inter-league game, brushed Vladi back with an eye-high fastball. There were many other highlights and lowlights. But September 29, 2004 was different. On that day, wearing an Expos cap purchased 30 years earlier, I left my apartment on the corner of Parc and St. Viateur (Jackie Robinson, I was later to learn, lived in the same building during his season with the Royals in 1946), rode the 80 bus south past the mountain, alighted downtown, and took the Metro eight stops to Olympic Stadium to see the last ever Expos home game. It says something about the sorry state of the franchise by that point that I was unable, from among my reasonably broad circle of friends, to find anyone who wanted to go with me. But there was no way I wasn't going to be there.

Arriving early gave me plenty of time to ponder the Big Owe, that concrete mistake on Pie IX. Built to the inscrutable dictates of a foreign architect who cared nothing for baseball and probably still snickers into his croissant at the mere thought of the game and its fans, *le Stade* does an amazingly thorough job of discouraging any sense of warmth or intimacy. It has always struck me as a building designed solely to look impressive from the perspective of a jet approaching the city, but even in that aim it fails, resembling, as it does, nothing so much as a gigantic futuristic toilet bowl.

On this day, though, I did my best to suppress such uncharitable thoughts and distill the essence of my 35 years as an Expos fan. In a nice gesture, the playing field had been opened to the public three hours before game time, and among countless affecting scenes of multi-generational homage I noted a curious sight: people of all descriptions were lying prostrate on the artificial turf, staring straight up, alone with their memories, seemingly attempting to get as close as possible to something they may not have been able to define. I tried it myself and found it special too, until the implications of artificial turf sunk in: we were lying in what amounted to a giant saliva/tobacco juice/sunflower seed shell receptacle. Yuk. Isn't one of the points of a carpet that it can be cleaned and vacuumed or something? I stood up.

As part of my general Keep It Positive! strategy, I had vowed to myself not to dwell on the spot I have come to think of as The Spot. Resistance was useless, however, and as if guided by a higher power I drifted over to a section of the right field fence between markers bearing the retired numbers of Rusty Staub and Andre Dawson. A handful of other stricken souls were already there, silent before this secular equivalent of the Wailing Wall. The fence had been moved in since that day in 1981, so it couldn't have been the exact spot, but it was close enough to impart a genuine gravitas to the moment. We didn't have to say anything. We probably shouldn't have. But like the baseball victims we so clearly were, we couldn't stop ourselves. We talked. And made things worse.

"Why the hell was Rogers on the mound? Has that ever been explained?"

"I think I read someplace that Reardon was too scared to go in."

"Fanning was never a real manager."

"Do you think Monday has any idea at all what he really did that day?"

It's just possible, I suppose, that not everyone reading this piece will know all the details, so I'll briefly synopsize. Rogers is Steve, a rookie hero on that first contending Expos team back in 1973, and by '81 long established as staff ace. Never a reliever, on the day in question he was strangely summoned to maintain a 1-1 tie in the top of the ninth inning and thus send the Expos into the bottom of the ninth with the chance to gain their first World Series berth. Reardon is Jeff, then the team's young bullpen stopper and the natural choice to have gone in. Fanning is Jim, the Expos GM and interim manager, who had the fantastic good fortune to be at the helm as the team made a stirring run to the NL East pennant, then a victory over the Phillies in a makeshift elimination series (1981 was a season split by a players' strike), and now to within a breath of the unthinkable. And Monday is Rick. Rick Monday hit a go-ahead home run off non-reliever Steve Rogers, who served him a hanging curve at the letters. The ball barely cleared The Spot, over the head of a despairing Andre Dawson. The Expos failed to tie it up in the bottom of the inning, and generations of Canadians were deprived of the opportunity to tell their grandchildren about the year the Expos met the Yankees in the Fall Classic.

Our ragged little band stood there by The Spot a minute or so longer. Then we dutifully allowed ourselves to be shepherded along with the rest of the faithful into the stands, where we watched our boys get soundly beaten by the Florida Marlins, a team that by perfect Expos symmetry was owned by the very man–I cannot bring myself to type his name–who had previously owned the Expos and given every appearance of trying to sabotage the franchise into non-existence. That man's upstart Marlins had pulled off a stunning World Series upset just a year earlier, defeating–yes– the New York Yankees. Typical. Typical. Typical. Termell Sledge, may his name liveth for evermore, made the final ever Expos home out.

The feeling I had, trudging out of Olympic Stadium on September 29, 2004, is a feeling that I sincerely hope you, dear reader, never have to feel. Our poor language is not up to the task of describing that feeling. The best word I can come up with is simply this: empty. I could not summon nostalgia, regret, wistfulness, resignation, righteous anger, any of those things. I just felt empty. Others must have too, because it was eerily quiet in that dank packed concourse.

I found my thoughts straying to the question, previously inconceivable, of whether I would remain a baseball fan. My team had always been the Expos, and I had just witnessed their death. As a child, the face that defined the game for me was Roberto Clemente's; the defining face of baseball today is Barry Bonds, a man whose character can be gauged by the fact that his teammates declined to leave the dugout and congratulate him when he passed Babe Ruth for second place on the all-time home run list. Was it time for me to make a clean break?

That line of thought was interrupted by the one image that sticks with me above all others from that day. Up ahead in the concourse, some sort of giveaway was going on: a scrum had formed around a group of stadium staff handing out posters. My eyes fell on a sensible-looking 40ish man–a man who, I suppose, was not dissimilar in many ways to me–fighting through the scrum with particular vigor. He got the poster and unscrolled it. What he saw was a tribute to the 1994 Expos: "Best Team in Baseball/*Meilleure Equipe en Baseball.*" (Except, of course, that they didn't get a chance to prove it, because 1994 was the season terminated by a strike in mid-August, and the dream lineup that was crushing the National League opposition—a young and fantastically talented team managed by Felipe Alou, a veteran of that distant '73 campaign—was sold off like smoke-damaged furniture that winter. How quintessentially Expos, that the organization would choose the day of the team's forced demise to taunt us with reminders of that ultimate outrage.)

The man who looked a lot like me stood there for a moment amid the throng, staring at his free souvenir poster. Then, calmly and methodically, he tore it into little pieces, tossed the scraps into the air, and walked off toward the Metro. I knew exactly how he felt.

If, on the other hand, they'd been giving away a 1973 team poster....

Swing and a Miss

At midnight, the sky had only four stars. Maddie stared up at them, her body spread like a starfish across the pitcher's mound. The humidity curled around her and the musty smell of the rain that was coming hung over her. Her knuckles were muddy from tears and dirt as she crushed a beer cap in her palm. The last bottle from her six-pack rested empty on her chest. She wore the Phillies batting helmet that Dan had bought her at their first game together. She gripped the empty beer bottle and swung at her head, making a popping sound against the helmet. Dan was already out of her life, and the season wasn't even close to over.

Maddie met Dan in the park. It was May. Maddie attended her first office softball meet as a spectator, blaming her inability to participate on a sudden bout of carpel tunnel. Dan was taking a walk in the park that night, and decided to sit in the stands and watch the game. He told Maddie that softball was for wussies, and then stood up from his seat to shout at her co-workers, "Hey, you freaky lame-o grapefruit slingers in walking shorts, you think softball's a real game?" Then he mumbled something to himself about a corporate team-building crap attack. Maddie hid her face in her hands and laughed. Dan told her that she was pretty, and asked if she liked baseball. She said, "Yes. In fact, I love it."

A week later, on a Monday night, the Phillies were playing against the Mets at home. Maddie hadn't been to a baseball game since she was 13 years old when her father took her and her brother to see the Phillies play at Veterans Stadium. As a kid, baseball games were about the bursts of salt in her mouth when she ate a giant pretzel as she watched the outfielders during the entire game. She would crunch her hands into fists and squint as she tried to follow the ball that seemed to be airborne forever. She held her breath each time an outfielder reached out to catch the ball, and it slid into his glove. The whole game froze for a second and then the teams switched places. Maddie's brother would poke her in the ribs and tell her to keep her eye on the guy on 3rd, or to wake up or she'd miss a homerun. But Maddie just stared into the outfield, a place where you could step back, watch, and wait until you caught a moment and held it in your hands. An outfielder could hold on to that sliver of time right before everything changes. Watching from the bleachers while sipping 7-Up to cut the pretzel salt that burned her lips was the closest that Maddie ever got to feeling like there are things that do last forever.

Dan told Maddie to meet him at Broad Street Subway, to just look for the bright yellow feathers. When Maddie exited the subway, Dan was pacing by the turnstiles, a foot taller than he was in the park, his eyes like shiny black screw heads peering out from beneath a red chicken beak. His body was adorned with hundreds of yellow feathers that ruffled slightly from the air currents that moved with the passing crowd. He clutched a long plastic horn and when he saw Maddie, he blew into it, startling some people walking by.

"This is for you," Dan said, handing the horn to Maddie, "unless you already have one that is."

"I had one," Maddie lied, "but my brother broke it the last time I lent it to him. This is perfect." She took the horn and looked into the mouth piece as though it were a kaleidoscope. "I see chickens fragmented into baseball diamonds and giant pretzels wearing mustard coloured coats."

"What the hell did you smoke on the subway?" Dan laughed, and grabbed the horn from Maddie. He puffed up his chest and blew into it again. Maddie cupped her ears to protect them from the noise. "C'mon, babe. We gotta a game to go to," Dan said, gripping her wrist and pulling her along as he ran.

They sat in the bleachers. Dan bought Maddie popcorn, a pretzel, and a beer. He complained about the Phillie Phanatic. He said that the Phanatic turned a quality baseball team into a gimmick. He was going to steal from the importance of good baseball by filling up game time with cheap stunts. The fans that were sucked into the show didn't give half a crap about baseball. They didn't understand what baseball was about. Maddie listened to Dan. His chicken feet were on the seat in front of him, and his feathered arms were folded across his feathered thighs. He didn't smile, or shout, or crack any jokes when he was talking. He just looked straight at her like he was asking her to stop the inevitable. She wanted to reach out, grab him by the feathers and whisper that she promised that good baseball would always take precedence over a bright green guy in a white and red pinstriped Phillies jersey, but instead she filled her palm with popcorn and pushed it into her mouth, nodding slowly enough to match his intensity.

Halfway through the first inning, Dan left his seat. He ran up and down the concrete steps and through the empty rows of seats. He shouted insults about the other team, as well as at the spectators who heckled him. Maddie didn't make out much of what he said. She watched the replay of a guy stealing second base on the video screen, and then an ad for Lays potato chips that was made up of thousands of little red and white lights on a black background. The occasional flash of Dan doing the chicken dance was captured on the replay screen, but Maddie soon switched her focus to the outfield, and waited. Between innings, Dan sat down next to her to catch his breath. He took a big gulp of beer, wiped his mouth with his feathers, saying, "Mind if I borrow this?" He grabbed the plastic horn that he'd given Maddie, and disappeared.

Maddie squinted at a large mass of yellow that appeared on top of the dugout. It sounded a horn, but the noise was swallowed by the stadium. It charged a furry mass of bright green wearing a Phillies jersey and red baseball socks. A close-up of Dan and the Phanatic was on the replay screen. The Phanatic swung his leg up to kick Dan, but fell flat on his back. Dan lept into flight, flapping his arms, his elbows pointed out like wing tips. He plummeted onto the Phanatic, and they rolled: green, yellow, green, yellow, green. The Phanatic got on his knees, straddling Dan. He threw his head back and pointed his horn-shaped snout to the sky. He clasped his floppy paws around Dan's throat and shook. The camera zoomed in on Dan's red beak that waved back and forth like an arrow on a broken scale. Then stadium security pulled Dan and the Phanatic apart. The Phanatic stood up with his legs in a wide stance, and raised his fists in victory. Dan, on the other hand, was dragged away by security. Maddie bought herself a 7-Up, and sipped. The player up at bat hit a pop-fly. She watched the ball's trajectory, how it rose up against gravity, paused in the air for an instant, and then plunged into the short-stop's glove. Maddie sipped and swallowed the suspended moment. The batter was out, and a new guy was up at bat.

In the sixth inning, Maddie got up to leave when Dan sat down in the seat next to hers with four hotdogs in a cardboard box, resting on top of a red Phillies batting helmet. He was no longer dressed like a chicken, but wearing jeans and a hooded sweatshirt.

"They confiscated my costume." He explained. "That asshole thinks he's better than everybody."

"Who? The security guard?" Maddie asked.

"No. That pussy, the Phanatic. Prick." Dan ate half a hotdog in one bite, and with his mouth full, offered one to Maddie. She grabbed it from the box.

"I'm sorry, but they took the horn too." Dan said, stuffing the second half of his hotdog in his mouth.

"It's okay."

"I got you this instead." Dan handed her the batting helmet.

"Thanks. It's really nice." Maddie said, trying it on.

Dan knocked on its surface and said, "You look good. And now you never have to worry about a head injury from a fly ball." He ducked in and kissed Maddie on the cheek.

The Phillies lost 5-3. Dan invited Maddie over to his place to watch the 11 o'clock news. He was pretty sure that he was going to make the sports highlights. They took the bus along Passyunk Avenue, and took turns wearing the batting helmet, knocking one another on the head and laughing about the ultimate fight between Dan and the Phanatic.

Dan's apartment was plastered with baseball posters. He had framed baseball cards of Mike Schmidt and Tug McGraw and a newspaper clipping of Pinky Whitney from the '30s on the wall. He had a full collection of bobble-head figurines lining his bookshelf, including one of the Phanatic. Dan threw himself down on the couch. He picked up a snow globe of Shibe Park from the coffee table and showed it to Maddie.

"Isn't this awesome?"

Maddie smiled and took the snow globe from Dan.

Dan stretched his legs out on the coffee table and turned on the TV. Maddie sat on the arm rest of the couch, cradling the snow globe in her palms and watched the tiny white flakes fall on Shibe Park as she slid off her flip-flops.

"Look, look, look. There I am. There I am." Dan shouted. "Phanatic, you asshole, looks like you're not the only one who can get a little airtime."

Maddie laughed. She watched Dan watch himself on television. It was the first time that she'd spent anytime with someone from outside her work crowd in over a year. Her co-workers spent most of their time outside of the office complaining about management and talking about their perfect visions of team building. Maybe Dan would know what she meant if she told him about the outfielders.

Dan got up from the couch and turned on the radio. "Cheesesteak Corner is the best radio show–" he said, "be back in a minute." He rushed out the room. Maddie put the television on mute and listened to "Cheesesteak Corner" on sports talk radio. She heard Dan shouting from the bedroom, and after a short delay, his voice, repeating what he had just said, came through clearly on the radio: "That's right. They confiscated my chicken costume and my horn. If this is how Citizens Bank security is going to treat Phillies' fans, you've gotta wonder why any one is showing up for games, Mike. I mean, we've gotta new stadium, but so what? It's obvious the Phanatic is smothering good baseball. This losing streak that we're on didn't come outta nowhere. The players are suffering, the fans are suffering. The morale is down and the Phanatic is making it worse. Someone outta run him down with the bullpen cart.... Thanks for your points, Dan."

Dan came back into the room. He was pacing while talking out loud about how he could buy a bear suit off the Internet, and that if he bought it that night, he could probably have it for the upcoming home game. He sat down at a small desk in the corner where he kept his computer. He called Maddie over to check out some of his potential bear suit options. Maddie leaned over his shoulder and asked him to click on a few images. She then suggested that he go with a chestnut coloured bear suit with an orange jersey and jumbo running shoes. She said that the orange would contrast with the Phanatic's bright green fur and that it would probably give Dan an edge that could overthrow the Phanatic. Dan stood up, grabbed Maddie by the t-shirt and kissed her.

The sun streaked across East Passyunk and South Seventh in low and bending rays. Maddie waited for the first rush hour bus. She stopped by her apartment to change her clothes for work. She hadn't slept yet.

The season progressed. June and July were thick with a losing streak, and Dan and Maddie's meetings became more frequent. They listened to away games on the radio, stretched out on his apartment floor, drinking beer in their underwear as the summer temperatures rose as high 106 degrees. Maddie didn't follow the games on the radio too well. She would just float with sound of the crowd that hummed around the announcer's voice. It sounded exactly like the ocean. It cooled her down in Dan's un-air conditioned apartment. She loved the spurts of silence over the airwaves and the richness of the announcer's tone when he said, "Swing and a miss." It made her feel the same way the outfielders did.

On a Friday night at the end of July, the Phillies lost against the Cubs. Maddie and Dan had too many beers. Dan sat at his computer, updating his baseball blog and Maddie lay on his floor in her underwear and batting helmet. She told Dan that it didn't matter that the Phillies lost because baseball made her feel like she could hold onto everything forever. She told him about the outfielders, the bursts of salt from the giant pretzels, and the sips of 7-Up. She told him about when she listened to the games on the radio, and the silence that built up before "swing and a miss."

Dan looked at her and laughed, "You look awesome in those panties and your batting helmet, but that is the freakiest thing I have ever heard anyone say about baseball."

Maddie lay still, her arm reached out across the floor, her fingers searching for her t-shirt.

"Well?" Dan said, "you don't think it's a little cuckoo?" He pulled Maddie towards him, and rolled on top of her. She thought of Dan blowing the long plastic horn in the subway, his chicken costume, how he ran through the empty rows of seats all alone and attacked the Phanatic on national TV. His rant on the radio. His search for the bear suit on the Internet. His obsessive preoccupation with his blog. She never once accused Dan of being the least bit unusual. He was just Dan. But Dan thought that she was a little cuckoo just for telling him something real about herself.

Suddenly, she felt like she did when she was listening to her co-workers discuss team-building over bad daiquiris: nodding in agreement, only half listening, never really in the moment. Not like those first few times she hung out with Dan, not like when she followed the trajectory of the ball into the outfield, not like the pending silence before the announcer says, "Swing and a miss."

I Really Need Ted Lilly to Throw the Hook

We're up two and I'm sick to death of losing.
It's Posada, never an easy out, but the hook
is there for Lilly, it's the seventh and his old team,
the $250-million fucking Yanks have beaten
shit out of us all week. And now, faced
with a real pitcher, they're driving up the count,
knowing its Speier or Ligtenberg or Frasor
to follow, who never seem to get a call, or
forgot how to pitch the minute they put on the
stupid new uniform. High fastball… strike. Change,
down the shoot, *whiff.* Fastball, fishing, off the plate.

And now I really need Ted Lilly to throw the hook.
It doesn't matter, but it's suddenly important now.

What I Don't Know About Baseball

I don't know anything about baseball.
But I know that my grandparents,
when not breeding award-winning Great Danes,
would sit in front of their wall of ribbons
in their respective but identical
Laz-e-Boys, surrounded by stacks of
remote controls and TV Guides
and, with Revenue Canada-like
statistic sheets, tick off in unison
whatever numbers they saw
in a pop fly to the second baseman
or a home run at the bottom of the ninth—
Where I saw a man hit a ball and run
they saw a formula, and scratched numbers
into their charts as methodically as astronomers
charting the wobble of the planets.

I do not know much about baseball
but I know that on the morning of my
first day of grade five, in a new town
(where for fun, I would hide
in the bushes on my lawn and
watch the Pakistani kids across the street
race their mosquito-like radio-controlled cars
around the neighbourhood)
my father tried to inaugurate me
to the world of athletics
by taking me to the abandoned lot

next to our prefab home
and pitching a Rawling's Softball
into my left eye.

I don't know baseball
but I know the fifth grader with a sleeveless
Randy "The Macho Man" Savage tee-shirt
and a slick, blond rat's tail
hanging down to his shoulder blades
(the first person my age I'd met in Mission BC)
wanted to fight me, because I had a black eye
and was from Quebec, or someplace.
In PE, while I was guarding him
on first base and Mrs. McGowen
was watching the pitch, he would lean over
and punch me in the stomach
then run off to second, as if it were all
just part of the play.

I don't know about baseball but I know
that the dugout, at Heritage Park Secondary school,
at roughly eleven thirty on a Wednesday night
when the dust is cold and the bench is tattooed
with the flaking scars of etched messages
such as "Sandra's a bitch" and "Darryl '95"
is a good place to get drunk off wine coolers
for the first and last time in your life.

I know the pitcher's mound is a good place
to get to second base with Melissa Wormsbekker
scrambling in the dust and cleat marks
knocking our teeth against each other,
lips numb, and faces wet with saliva,
till we curl into each other
motionless, breathless,
and afraid of third base,
a tight knot in the middle of the diamond
hiding under the charted wobble of the planets.

Rapture & the Big Bam

Transported by trifles these soupy days–bright-blooming
paprika yarrow, that bagpiped out-of-tune *Auld lang syne*
tumbling over bone-dry hills, my son trembling with bliss

& dread as he plummets down the frog-slide's tongue–
I grow wary of my own whirligig bouts of delight
when I find myself sideswiped by a ball of electrical tape

made, the plaque claims, by Babe Ruth at St. Mary's School for Boys.
Needless to say, who cares? Why pause for even a moment
before this misshapen chotchka on a Plexiglas shelf? Relic-like,

under a hard light's glare, beside Cobb's sharpened cleats
& Clemente's jersey from such & such a game, it was a wad
of nothing, really, a lopsided sphere most likely never used

for a game or even shagging flies & is only one more piece
of the past's lumpish fruit turned artifact behind alarmed glass.
And still, why pretend the wondrous & the useless weren't the same

all along? The meaningless, the miraculous–who are we to say?
Picture this tight bundle sailing past each backpedaling-boy
history swallowed whole, long past the orphanage wall-notch

marking Brother Mathias' furthest shot, past that rusted boiler
& the harbor's rotting hulls, & past now even what legend will allow
as it soars beyond his Pigtown two-room shack with its avalanche

of bottles & chairs & his sauced-up father prowling again, back
from a day of door-to-door lies about his worthless lightning rods,
flames, guarantees, God's wrath. Or at least this is how

it might have seemed. Rapture, *raptura: to carry away
with joy;* earlier: *to kidnap, rape,* although for better or worse
in this simmer of pleasure no one's talking etymology here.

In the last year Ruth played for the Sox, he pummeled
a slider off Columbia George for the longest home run ever hit.
With ease. Without much of anything but a body-thrashing stroke

during spring training when, as if it were possible, all of this
means even less. Billy Sunday, ex-right-fielder-turned-preacher-ablaze,
taking a break from bellowing about the Devil's spitballs

& ways to head-butt sin, watched that ball beeline for even more
empty sky & for as long as this fast-winging shape remains
aloft, & even for a bit longer still, it's the only grace

Sunday or anyone could feel, buoying them beyond the far wall
& revival tent pitched across the field, the bay's abandoned shipyards,
all the dead that year from flu. Or is that too much to presume?

Even if perfection here means a split-second thwack & all
the countless ways to be held in thrall are both our shame & luck,
it matters little just now. I tell you no one could help their joy.

Cro!

When I found the Samurai Bears getting ready to play in the Long Beach Armada's Golden Baseball League home opener at old Blair Field, they'd already lost 11 of 12 games, had been told not to return to a handful of motels after ruining a series of SouthWestern bathtubs, were shuttling ten hours at a time through the 90 plus summer heat in an old coach with a beaten up VCR, and had sandpapered their manager's ass—Warren "Cro" Cromartie, the old Expo—to the point that he'd grown exasperated with the task of teaching twenty young Japanese ballplayers the finer points of Yankee Ball. When I found him shaking his head on the top lip of the Armada's visitors' dugout, Cro groused that his young players didn't hustle or think the game right or were too busy styling for the American Britneys in the stands to score more than two runs a night. When I asked about one player—who turned out to be the owner's son—sulking by himself in left field during batting practice, Cro held up a finger and announced to me in bold tones as if addressing the UN General Assembly: "In Japan, the managers hit you, they slap you, they kick you, they carve you up! And these guys got a problem with me?" Just then, an errant throw from the field landed at my feet, but when I went to pick up the ball, Cro broadcast, "Lookit that! Can't even keep the object of their attention on the motherfuckin field!" before staring with disgust at his sorry-armed charges, who didn't know whether to retrieve the ball or consider that long swim back to Tokyo.

Cro had sworn that he'd never return to baseball as a manager, but all of that changed the night Nick Belmonte found him eating at the Macaroni Grill. Cro liked Italian food—had a fetish for it, he said—and that's why Belmonte and his elderly mother found him where they did. Nick had just got off the phone with Kevin Outcalt, who'd been approached by the organizers of the Golden Baseball League, who rhapsodized about skydiving managers and falcons delivering the first pitch to the mound and a barnstorming all-Japanese team coached by an ex-big leaguer who could tell his *sushi* from his *sashimi*. Cro looked up from his plate to see Nick and the old woman staring at him, but before he could return their bug eyes, the son spoke: "Warren Cromartie? I've been searching for you, man." Nick didn't seem like a ghost from the game that Cro had left behind in 1991–his last year of pro ball–at least not under the plastic vine and grape baubles of the restaurant. But it only took Cro a few seconds to realize that, in that very moment, his baseball past–the scrappy Florida sandlots, the green baize of Montreal's Olympic Stadium, his wild times as a Tokyo Giant–had gathered into the present–Miami, where he'd lost his oceanfront palace, got divorced, suffered bad investments, survived two heart attacks, coached kids for scratch, worked on occasional TV and radio spots, and now this: fetish night at the Macaroni Grill.

Nick Belmonte talked about the Samurai Bears. He told Cro about this team of young Japanese ballplayers who were going to become the first Asian team to compete in the USA since Waseda University toured the country 100 years ago. The Bears had been dreamed up by the GBL to play against suburban Southwestern teams in Yuma, Chico, Long Beach, and other places, replacing an all-Mexican team who dropped out after their ballpark was seized by government authorities at the behest of a rival team. Nick told Cro that he was the right guy to manage them–after all, he'd played 7 years for the Tokyo Giants, had led them to the Japanese World Series, appeared on game shows, hustled Yaka Soba noodles and Kirin lager, and prowled the town with two Sumo wrestlers, Takamiya and Konishiki, as his wingmen–but Cro just laughed at those memories and got back to his food. A few days later, Nick was renting a car in Tampa when the woman behind the counter noticed Nick's ballcap and told him that her daddy was a ballplayer, too, a former Expo who'd played in Tokyo. Cro called Nick and told him to lay off working on his daughter, because the thought of all those long bus rides and bad burgers and indie ball in shit towns he'd never heard of were for hamburger-assed oldtimers desperate for a taste of the game, not *osamas* with their own weekly radio show presented by Chivas Regal.

But last June, as I rode with Cro and the Bears from the soft sands of Long Beach to the cow pastures south of Chico–10 hours through the rain to northern California–the 1974 National League Rookie of the Year runner-up confessed: "When Nick Belmonte approached me, my life was at a standstill. That night at the restaurant, baseball came and found me; Japan came and found me. I knew what I had to do. I knew I had to give it back," he said, braiding his fingers together and widening those bright Satchmo eyes. Sitting behind him on the bus, the Bears–at 22 average years of age, the youngest team in America's newest independent league–pounded melon cream sodas, iPodded hip hop and stared out the window waiting for another town to appear on the horizon. The Bears were unlike any team in baseball not only because of their nationhood, but because they were nomadic, itinerant. Formed in haste to fill in for the Mexicans, the Bears were homeless, forced to play 80 away games. On occasion, Cro liked to pontificate, "We are the stepchild of the league, used and abused!" but it was his job to shepherd the Bears from nowhere to somewhere.

The Bears were recruited and organized in under two months. Because a lot of Japanese ballplayers have been weeded out of American minor league ball due to recent changes to H2B visas, over 100 ballplayers heeded the Golden League's call for try-outs. The Bears invited 40 players to stay on, but brought only fifteen across the Pacific. Because of further visa problems–many of them were travelling using student visas–they arrived in Yuma, Arizona, for the final week of spring training as the youngest (and least experienced) team in the league. This is to say nothing of the fact that, while nary a single player would acknowledge it, the Bears were 2005's WorldBall poster boys, ersatz Ichiros in a modern era when player exchange between Asian, Latin American, North American, Australian, and EuroBall nations at all levels has never been more involved.

Every Bear had their own reason for playing in America. Blair Sly, the team's director of operations, told me that the team was divided among "those who think this is a team of Japanese players learning to play American ball, and those who think this is a visiting Japanese team playing in America." Some of the players were less rooted in J-Ball than others. Hideki Nagasaka, who'd been brought in to reinforce the Bears' roster, dressed head to toe in vintage San Diego Padres' B-boy gear with headphones perpetually strapped to his head. He'd played baseball in Japan until he was 19, but quit after he being slapped one too many times by his manager. "The coaches in Japan forced me out of baseball, even though I was as good as any other player. They hit me every day and treated me like garbage," he said, disgusted at the memory. Nagasaka left the game for three years and became a deejay—he was known as DJ Hide-Key in the nightclubs of Yokohama City—and boasted of owning 15,000 albums. He joined the Bears because "he wanted to play real baseball with real baseball players," but complained that "a lot of my team-mates can't get their heads out of Japan. As far as I'm concerned, I came here to play fucking American baseball, not some weak Japanese version of the sport."

Like Nagasaka, Kazuhiro Kono, a stocky, veteran outfielder with gold-streaked hair who wore number one, had also been a promising teenager playing high school ball in Japan. As an 18 year-old, his team from Meitoku High faced Hideki Matsui's school, the first time the two greatest Japanese teenagers had played each other in a nationally-televised championship game. In one of the most famous moments in Japanese youth ball history, the camera swung in on Kono as he prepared to pitch to Matsui for the fifth time, having been ordered to walk the future Yankee slugger in his first four at-bats. Kono looked into the dugout for amnesty, but his manager refused to allow him to pitch to Matsui. When the future Samurai Bear gathered himself into his wind-up, tears were streaming down his face. A few months later, the young star was passed over in the Japanese pro draft, having disgraced himself and his team. Matsui was drafted number one; we all know what happened to him. Kono went to Senshu University, where he tore apart pitchers, but was ignored in the subsequent draft even though his manager had been dismissed over his tactics. Blackballed in his homeland, not a single scout would look at him, at least not until the Golden Leaguers staged their tryout camp.

For Kono, the GBL was his major league.

Over the first few weeks of the season, three of the Bears had gone home and two had split with their girlfriends. One of the players woke Blair Sly at 6:30 in the morning and asked to be driven from the motel to Long Beach airport after paying for his room with the last of his American money. Another player walked into the women's washroom at a truck stop, unable to read the signs. Sly had received complaints from hotels that their bathtubs had been damaged, but this was only because the players were using them to wash the hot pots and rice cookers they'd brought in two big suitcases from home. Washrooms became the de facto kitchens in most rooms, but the Bears discovered that not every town had stores selling sesame oil or teriyaki sauce. One player, Wesley Yazzie, told me: "In some cities, the good shops are downtown, but because we stay on the outskirts and don't have a lot of money, it's prohibitive to take cabs to get there to buy the food. For awhile, the guys were doing this, but there was no money left to buy the things we needed."

The gulf between Cro and his charges wasn't actually as wide as the old bugger made it seem. If any player had known the disaffection of playing in foreign lands, Cro had. After 17 years as a professional, Cro had played more baseball outside America than in it. He'd been a Montreal Expo for nine years and a Tokyo Giant for seven (he spent his last year with the Kansas City Royals). He'd married a Quebecois woman, and had spurned the San Francisco Giants for Tokyo, who threw scads of money at him. Cro had spent years watching television in languages he couldn't understand, trying weird food he couldn't name, getting on the wrong buses, leaving family behind, and arguing long-distance with his wife. In one instance, he stepped in the toilet after climbing out of his shoebox shower in his shoebox apartment in Tokyo before turning to the wall and shouting at the deep nothing: "What the fuck am I doing?" On that long bus ride to Chico, Cro told me: "In life, you make sacrifices, and you live with them. You have to be who you're going to be and nothing can stop that. When I signed with the Giants, my wife said, 'This is probably going to break up our marriage.' And she was right. It did."

Cro liked to talk about how life is a circle. He'd been one of the first black American ballplayers to bring the style and swang of the major leagues to Japan, and now twenty young Japanese kids were coming back to learn about it for themselves: this was a circle. His first AAA Expo team—the one that fed the '76 Expos with nine full-time call-ups, Hawk Dawson and Jerry White among them—were called the Bears; this was a circle, too. He'd been best friends with Geddy Lee of Rush ever since the band had invited him down to Morin Heights Studio outside of Montreal, where Cro got to hear the "Tom Sawyer" master tapes cranked over the studio speakers. A few days later, Cro asked Geddy to come out and see the Expos play, and he hit the game-winning home run, but he forgot about Geddy in all his excitement, leaving his friend waiting outside the door. Still, Geddy kept his tickets and flew to Tokyo to see Cro's last game in Japan, and, in Long Beach, the public address system played "Fly By Night" over the speakers: a circle. And when John Bell showed up at Blair Field to watch the Bears play, you could have poked Cro with a Kit Kat and he would have fallen over.

John Bell was working at the New Otani Hotel in Los Angeles in 1984 when he saw Cro cross the floor of the lobby. He went up and told him he was a fan, so Cro, who was one day removed from leaving for Japan, invited him for a drink (it turned out that Cro did a lot of this in his time; a writer from Montreal who was doing a story on the team remembered being a teenager driving up Crescent Street with her girlfriends, and Cro trying to hitch a ride with them to the bar). Since John had played high school ball in Japan, he told Cro what to expect from the fans, the press, the stadia. John remembers that "Cro was really nervous. You could tell that he was wondering whether he was doing the right thing, rejecting the majors in his prime to play for a lot of money in this faraway place." Cro got on the plane the next morning, and after 7 years, Sadaharu Oh, the Babe Ruth of Japan and coach of the Giants, sent Cro home with these words: "You have mastered the Japanese game." And now here he was, trying to get kids from Kyoto thirty years his junior to slap the outside pitch down the line with a runner on second instead of automatically throwing out their bat to bunt, the same kind of awkward adjustment he'd had to make as a *wakai senshu* in his prime.

Yes, a circle.

After watching the Bears play, you could tell that the players were gifted, but that they were having a hard time breaking old habits. All Japanese ballplayers are taught the same approach to the game. Their baptism is uniform and systematic. They learn to groom and till the field before they're allowed to hold a bat, and when they do, they're taught situational baseball rather than to react instinctively within the at-bat. Cro liked to complain that they didn't know the inside game–how to read a pitcher's tendencies, how to study flaws in the opponents' game and communicate them to team mates. When I asked why this was, he elucidated: "Because no one in Japan talks! The dugouts there, man, they're quieter than a tomb." Watching the Bears, it was obvious that their rhythm of the game was unique; they played base-to-base, batter-to-batter, rarely swung for the fences, and didn't attack the basepaths. Still, it would have been difficult to expect too much too soon from the Bears, especially considering that their diet, game day routine, language and culture had made a 180 degree turn in a matter of weeks. They were required to fight through every day, then fight through every game.

Against the Long Beach Armada, a record crowd of 3,300 filled Blair Field; almost half of them were Japanese American. Under the venerable blue corrugated roof of the old park, the Bears stood along the first base line for another home opener that wasn't their own and watched as the Consul General of Japan threw out the first pitch, Los Angeles Dodgers president Peter O'Malley spoke, and the *taiko* drummers drummed before giving way to the two anthems of the competing teams. While the Bears kept the score close (they would eventually succumb 5-4 for their 13th loss in 15 games), I combed the stands and discovered that almost every Japanese-American in attendance had had relatives interned, or had been interned themselves, in California during the Second World War. One fellow, George Nakataki, told me he was shipped to Arkansas when he was thirteen. He said that there'd been collecting points not far from the field, and that he'd played lots of baseball and softball with his friends at the camps. When I asked him what he thought the Bears symbolized, and whether their tour carried added weight considering what had happened in this part of the world in the past, he told me, "My father, who's dead now, couldn't believe that someone like (Hideo) Nomo had made it to the major leagues, so I can't imagine what he'd think of this. I suppose it says something about the power of sports, and how it leaps over a lot of that stuff. A lot of Japanese people are proud of this team, and, I don't know if you've noticed, but the loudest cheers seem to happen whenever they do something good."

Support for the Bears didn't only come from the Japanese-American fans gathered above the visitors' dugout, but from Armada supporters, too. In Yuma, Arizona—a stone's throw away from Gila River, one of the largest internments camps of the Second World War—fans had descended into the concourse in the middle innings and traded in their hometown colours for Bears caps and paraphernalia, then crossed the stands en masse to throw their support behind the visitors. They probably did this because of the puckish and spirited nature of the Bears' play, but it didn't hurt having that jabberjaw Cro hold court in the third base coach's box, where he kibbitzed with fans, asking their opinion on whatever song happened to be playing over the PA at the time, and did they like Cozy Powell or Simon Phillips or that thumper from Mountain, and what about my man John from Led Zeppelin, that dude had a 24 inch bass drum!

Because the Bears' Long Beach motel was in close proximity to an Asian market, they were able to load up on ramen noodles, miso soup, Japanese curry and rice, a culinary adjustment that, after awhile, seemed to help the Bears' find their form. At first, Game Two looked a lot like the beginning of Game One, with the teams tied 2-2, but the Japanese-American fans seemed to help the Bears find their focus and purpose. Roving throughout the crowd, I spotted a young woman with long black hair and a Japanese novel folded open across her lap. Her name was Mai, and she was Yuji Ishida's girlfriend, having just flown over from Japan. When I told Mai that maybe what her boyfriend and his team needed was a lucky charm, she buried her face in her hands to hide her embarassment. But when Yuji lumbered to the plate with the game tied and a runner on second in the late innings, you could sense that something was about to give.

Yuji looked over a few pitches, ground his back heel into the dirt, and slugged an inside pitch that spiked the icing sugar down the line. At once, the field exploded in a miasma of firsts: the first clutch, go-ahead (and later, winning) hit in the Bears' short history; the first time the quiet Japanese players on the bench had exploded into any kind of wild cheering; the first winning streak by an Asian team on American soil (the Bears would win the next evening, too–in extra innings, no less– and the game after that); and the first time anyone in California had witnessed the Banzai Cheer, Cro's celebratory post-home run conniption. Clapping out a busy syncopation, he stood before the team and chanted "BANZAI!!" while waving his arms like a fat duck trying to fly. The cheer had become commonplace during Cro's run in Tokyo, and was now the Bears' expression of joy on the green fields of their new land.

In the stands, Mai was ecstatic; so were the rest of the fans. The scene would have been perfect had I not spotted Kono the veteran sitting on the dugout steps during the cheer, and then disappearing into the clubhouse. Cro had benched Kono for the series. He'd been a late-inning defensive replacement and his three at-bats saw him standing at the plate, bewildered with his bat on his shoulder. Cro said that it was no accident that the team had turned it around in Kono's absence. "He wants to go up there and be Barry Bonds. He wants to flex like a big shot, but he's hitting a buck fifty," said Cro. "He doesn't warm-up right, doesn't try. He runs the count to 3-0 and wants the sign to swing away. I don't give it to him, so he steps out, keeps waiting for what he ain't gonna get. His ass is going home," said Cro, firmly. When Blair and one of the coaches approached Kono after the game and suggested that he talk to Cro, maybe apologize to him and straighten things out, the veteran *sempai* told them, proudly: "I'm not saying shit to Cro. He is disrespectful and he should be apologizing to me."

The next morning, when I climbed the bus bound for Chico, things went from bad to worse for Kono, who was nowhere to be seen. He eventually got on, but not before Cro undressed him in front of his team-mates, made him carry his heavy luggage down the narrow aisle, and told him to sit at the back of the bus, where he stared out the rain-specked window at the rolling nothing of the road. "Stud's going home," growled Cro before settling into his seat and drawing "Exit, Stage Left" from his CD pouch.

The ride to Chico was achingly long. The team stopped at Jack-in-the-Box for lunch. Cro said, "I can't eat this shit, but what're you going to do? These guys got no money." We looked around at the young, sleepy-eyed Japanese men trying to get around on their burgers, and it was hard not to feel for them. Still, because the journey was propelled by two victories in Long Beach–they would win in Chico, too, and discover no less than three Japanese restaurants in the area–there was little heaviness to the team's mood, with the exception of Kono, who slouched in the depths of the bus, a satellite disappearing from view. After 7 or 8 hours, Cro grew tired with the ride and blunted the boredom by riffing for the last three hours of the trip: "Big man, we gotta get us a plane, this ain't right! We gotta schlep our funky-assed feet so that some investor can save a little money?!? No, sir! Lookit all this nothing out there: whatta dump. I could never fucking live here in Dorothyland, in Totoland. Fuckin Lassie territory, man. Walter! Walter! That motherfuckin windscreen's gonna crack apart and stick your ass to that chair of yours, Walter!"

Me, Blair and Walter (the bus driver) encouraged Cro with gales of laughter, and after awhile, you could hear ripples coming from the kids behind us. Even though most of them couldn't understand Cro's words or his humour, they knew that their Skip was on a roll, and that even though he was pissed, he was good-pissed, something they'd never seen before in any of their other managers. "Fuckin skanky assed motherfuckers," he'd say, gazing back at his team. "Look at them. Sorry, bastards. They don't have a home, none of 'em." After crossing from Yuba City into Chico ("Whatta fuckin dump. Blow it up. I could NEVER live here!"), Walter the driver found the hotel. Pulling into the parking lot, there was a sign staring at The Bears from the front of the Holiday Inn:

WELCOME AMERICAN LEGION BASEBALL

Cro buried his face in his hands and pretended to cry. For the first time, he was glad that his boys had no clue.

How to Throw a Kick-Ass Tailgate Party

Put on every bit of clothing you own
with your team's logo on it.
I mean everything.
It's impossible to go overboard here.
Face paint in your team's colours
is a nice touch.
Body paint is even better.

Decorate your pickup truck, van, or SUV,
with paint, flags, and stickers.
Leave no nook and cranny undecorated.
Windows especially.
Poor visibility
is a small price to pay
for team spirit.

Portable radios belong in the Stone Age.
Get a friend to bring their HD Plasma TV
(with an extra long extension cord)
and set it on top of your vehicle
to keep track of all pre-game interviews
and the other games
going on in North America.

Pack coolers with hamburgers and hotdogs to grill
and, of course, beer.
Go for big game like grizzly bear and moose
if you're feeling adventurous.
Pigeon and squirrel meat are also tasty alternatives.
Live by the zoo?
Hey, the possibilities are endless....

Portable and store bought grills are for sissies.
Pack your handmade BBQ grill
made from left over NASA shuttle parts.
You'll be barbecuing like the astronauts.
Don't forget to siphon the liquid hydrogen fuel,
it'll give your grillables
that certain *je ne sais quoi*!

The Game

June. Afternoon. They march toward the baseball diamond.
The sun is sinking. Risk of thunderstorms.

A gray wind disturbs the trees.
In the leaves, butterflies kneel in prayer.

Praying for shelter, wings in spasms
like mouths of saints speaking in tongues. A plea to ward off rain.

Still, they march.
Heads bowed, wooden bats nestled and heavy on their shoulders.

The procession marches toward the dusty field.
To play the game before night comes.

Before lampposts lift themselves from the ground,
leaving crumbs of light for the players to find their way home.

Alternative Careers for Former Expos Mascot "Youppi!" Should His Stint with the Montreal *Canadiens* Not Work Out

Seeing eye monster

Motivational speaker

Co-hosting Regis & Youppi!

Elmo's kooky uncle on Sesame Street

Stunt double for McDonald's Grimace

Contestant in Dancing With the Stars

Disgruntled union president for furry mascots

Bodyguard for former child star Corey Feldman

Make a comeback in "Revenge Flick" directed by Tarentino

Stark County Baseball

Right from the start, I didn't want to do the reading at the Stark Public Library in Stark County, Ohio, which, as anyone from there will tell you, is a straight shot down Route 77 from Cleveland where I live. It's a quick hour. This is the kind of thing they say in Stark County, Ohio with about the same frequency as they say, in other parts of the world, that it looks like rain.

I was promised that if I got there early I'd get a tour of the Football Hall of Fame, which is the jewel of Canton, Ohio, smack dab in the center of Stark County. It was Wendell Horn, President of the Friends of the Stark County Public Library who made this offer, when he called to ask me to come to read. The other thing he said was that he had heard that I was a lot of fun. This was something that another writer had said about me, apparently when she'd been down in Stark County to read herself.

"A lot of fun," said Wendell Horn on the phone. "That was all I needed to hear."

I told him I'd be there for the reading. "All the same," I said, "I think I'll skip the tour of the Football Hall of Fame."

"I see," said Wendell.

"I mean, if it's OK by you."

"No problem."

Then he told me that, instead of inside the Stark County Public Library, I would be giving my reading outside—at the Stark County Ballpark.

"Don't you worry," he told me. "We're wired."

"That's good," I said.

"I mean for sound," he said.

"You know what," I said. "Why don't we just have it in the library?"

When I said this Wendell Horn just laughed.

By the time it was time for the reading, the snow was gone. It was springtime in Ohio, which, next to the fall, is the best time of year here. As I drove the straight shot along Route 77 on my way out of

Cleveland I allowed myself to think that it wasn't going to be that bad. I've discovered this is the kind of thing you say to yourself when you're a writer, when you're on the way to a reading. I read somewhere about Balzac giving a reading atop a large block of cheddar cheese, and that Mordecai Richler had telecast a whole series of CBC interviews from inside a Remi Martin bottle. Hell, if Richler could allow himself to be locked into a glass prison, who was I to complain about driving out to Stark County or reading outside? It was a straight shot from Cleveland, after all. There were versions of the story about Richler in which it was Richler's idea to read from inside the liquor bottle. If they wanted me to read at a baseball park, I told myself, I'd read at a goddamn baseball park. I'd stand on the mound, for all I cared and belt it out into the stands. If they wanted me to chew tobacco, I'd chew it. Then I'd get my check and I'd get the hell out of there. As I drove, I tried my best to manufacture what I believed would have been Richler's attitude toward the whole thing which was, more or less, to know the whole thing was ridiculous, and to do it anyway.

The baseball park was about a mile and a half off the highway, just east of Stark Tires, across the street from a wrecked and dilapidated movie theatre. Wendell Horn was there waiting for me just inside the entrance to the stadium, standing exactly where he promised he would.

"I'm Steve Hayward," I told him.

"It's a real pleasure, Dr. Hayward," he said. The way he said doctor had a bit of a sneer in it. It reminded me of the way my mother said it, out of the corner of her mouth, as if to say it wouldn't be the worst thing in the world if one of her kids turned out to be a real doctor instead of having a so-called doctorate in English literature. "Any trouble getting here?"

"None at all," I told him.

"So the map worked?"

"The map was excellent," I said, and then with that giddiness that sometimes descends upon a literary unknown like myself when he finds himself a guest of honor, I heard myself adding, a moment later, "It was one of the best maps I've seen."

It was, I see now, too much. Whatever else can be said about him, Wendell Horn was no fool; he was a tall man with white, elaborately trimmed eyebrows, and he knew when he was being condescended to. It startled him. Though Canton is just an hour south of Cleveland, there's a distinct twang in people's accents that's unheard in the bigger city, which reminds you aren't far from West Virginia and Kentucky. There is also a kind of Southern gentility down there, a timeworn conviction that civility is a cardinal virtue. Though I tried to make light of it, tried, as it were, to retract the comment, it was too late. Wendell had already changed his mind about me. I suppose I know for a fact that what happened next didn't only happen because of that single moment of ill-considered sarcasm, or that the Stark County Library changed their plans when they found themselves confronted by an ironic Canadian like myself, but it didn't help. Whatever the case may be, it was at that moment I noticed Wendell Horn was wearing a baseball uniform. Before I could comment on it, though, he took a step backwards, looked at me, and shook his head, and this is what he said: "You're not going to pitch in that."

I was dressed the way authors are supposed to dress: in black jeans, a black t-shirt, black sports coat, and shiny black shoes.

"Pitch?" I said.

Once again, Wendell Horn just laughed.

As if it were a medieval church in a medieval town in the south of France, the baseball diamond behind the Stark County Library was the most splendid thing about Stark County. The lights snapped on as Wendell and I came in through a small door in the right field fence and veritably glinted off the backstop, reflecting toward the sky the immaculate green of the turf, the immaculate blue of the home run fence. Unlike most other ballparks I had been to in Ohio, where advertisements of all sorts are stuck everywhere it is plausible or possible to do so, the home run fence at the Stark County Ballpark was an unpolluted vista, virgin territory.

"Is this heaven," I said, "or is this Ohio."

"Ohio," said Wendell Horn.

"That's from *Field of Dreams*," I said. "You know, with Kevin Costner in it."

"I don't know it."

"It's by a Canadian," I told him. "W. P. Kinsella, I mean, the book that came before the movie–actually it was a story first. Anyway, he's a Canadian."

"You know," said Wendell Horn. "I did *not* know that. But I don't know the movie, as I said. I don't care much for movies about the game. I care for the game, if you catch me."

"Actually, Kinsella's from Manitoba," I said. I didn't even know if that was true. I had no idea where he was from. It made sense that he was from somewhere out West, but maybe it was all the way out west. "Yes," I said, rambling, "He's as Canadian as the day is long."

By this time Wendell Horn had stopped listening to me. We were now at the pitcher's mound, where I found myself looking at the whole of the Stark County Library Board, who were sitting on a bench in the dugout, impatiently, like kids waiting to be put into a game.

"Well," said Wendell Horn, then, pressing a baseball into my hand. "Let's see what you're made of, Mr. Baseball Writer."

I realized then that he had left me standing on the mound. "What's going on?"

"What's going on," jeered one of the octogenarians on the bench. He was completely bald, and for some reason speaking in a high falsetto voice.

"I thought I was giving a reading," I said. "From my novel."

"From my novel," echoed the old man again, still in his falsetto.

The rest of the old men on the bench laughed their heads off.

"I don't know why you're laughing," I said.

This made them laugh more. Some of them were so old and laughing so hard that I wondered if it might kill them. I should have left then. I should have driven back to Cleveland, picked up my wife and kids and put them into the car and kept driving, all the way north, back to Toronto. But we had a mortgage and one of the kids had a cold and I needed the money. "Listen," I said. "I don't know what is going on here, but I don't think it's very funny."

This stopped no one.

"Come on, Mr. Baseball Writer," said Wendell Horn. "Let's see what you're made of."

"Flesh and bone," I said. "Like anyone."

"You wish," shouted a different one of the old guys on the bench.

"You wish," said another one of the guys to the first one.

Then everyone laughed like hell again.

"Let me tell you," said Wendell Horn, swinging the bat over the plate. "Your book isn't bad, for being a book."

"Well," I said, lamely. "It *is* a book."

"Listen," he said. "I'm president of the Stark County Library Board. I can tell a book when I see one."

"I'm leaving," I said.

Wendell Horn seemed to know I was just bluffing. "Maybe you can write," he said. "But you know nothing about baseball."

"It's a work of fiction," I told him.

Wendell Horn hoisted the bat to his shoulder. "Go ahead," he said.

"I'm not going to do this," I said.

"I'm not going to do this," said the old guy with the falsetto voice. Maybe it was his real voice, I found myself thinking, maybe he just talks like that.

"Really," I said. "I mean, I mean it."

"Really," whined the guy on the bench.

"What're you worried about," said Wendell Horn. "I'm an old man."

"I'm an old man," called out the guy on the bench in the falsetto voice. Then, a moment later a deeper voice, "Sorry Wendell."

"One pitch and I get my check and go–deal?"

"Deal," he said.

"I have your word?"

"Shut up and pitch," he told me.

And so I got ready. I took off my jacket, and I stretched a little. I worked my right shoulder and I flexed my fingers. I was taking a long time and I knew it, and I could tell that several of the old men on the bench were beginning to fall asleep. One of them got up to relieve himself. And then, in much the same way that a single yawning person is supposed to create the need to yawn in those around him, the rest of the men on the bench got up to relieve themselves. They did this by stepping into the semi-darkness of the field's edge, as if there were no choice about it and there weren't bathrooms somewhere inside the stadium, just a few feet away. I took my time, thinking that Wendell Horn could not be immune, but he was.

"I can wait all night," he told me. "I've had a colostomy."

Seeing there was no choice, I went into my windup. I suppose that in the version of this story they'll tell at my funeral, I will lob a soft underhand pitch toward Wendell Horn, a pitch that anyone, even the guys who have had colostomies, can knock clear over the right field wall. In that version of this story, I will watch the ball sail over my head and smile at the vagaries of human existence with a benign acceptance of it all. Or at least, I will not throw a knuckleball. I will, instead, throw a fastball. Or some approximation of it. A slow fastball that Wendell Horn can knock over the right field fence and I'll go over to shake his hand. He'll hand me a check and I'll go back to my normal life as a writer who knows nothing about baseball, really. This story will have a happy ending.

But this is what really happened:

I did throw a knuckleball, which I should not have done because, in the first place, I wanted Wendell Horn to hit the ball, and, in the second place, it isn't one of the pitches I have, so to speak, in my arsenal. It was a pitch I had read about it. I had taken out books from the library, and seen the pictures, and had even tried holding a baseball in my hand in the way I might have if I was going to throw a knuckleball. But I had not thrown one before. It was a theoretical pitch as far as I was concerned.

I regretted it the moment it left my hand. Though I began to regret it more when I saw that Wendell Horn knew I was going to throw a knuckleball, as if there was someone in the back of the stadium with my stats who had run those numbers through a computer and signaled to Wendell that he should be ready for a knuckleball–and for that reason Wendell horn stepped forward and got ready to bunt.

And bunt he did, laying it down perfectly on the third base line. It was lovely to see, though if there had been a catcher there is no question that he would have been out at first, for he was an old man with a colostomy bag, the kind of guy who never could run very quickly to begin with and now could hardly run at all. But there was no catcher and I lunged forward, fielded the ball myself and sprinted like hell after Wendell Horn. As slow as he was moving, he was nearly at first base by the time I caught up to him. I'd like to be able to say that I didn't dive to make the out, but I did. I hit the old man with such force that we both fell to the ground just beyond first base.

"Safe," called a voice.

I looked around, not sure who was speaking or where the voice was coming from.

"Safe," said the voice again, and out of the shadows stepped the ghost of Mordecai Richler.

"Holy cow," I said.

"Holy cow?" said the ghost of Mordecai Richler. "I come back from the dead and this is the most you can manage." It was not a question.

"Sorry," I said.

"And now you're apologizing," said the ghost.

"Sorry," I began to say again, then stopped. "I love your work," I said. "I mean, you're such an inspiration."

"Inspiration," snorted Mordecai Richler's ghost. "Let me tell you, it's no picnic."

"Sorry to hear that," I said.

It was then that I noticed that Wendell Horn had got up off the grass. He dusted himself off and, like a true gentleman, walked over and gave me the check. "A real pleasure," he said, and made me promise that if I ever found myself in Stark County that I would look him up. A kind of jubilant feeling came over me, and on our way out to the parking lot I asked the ghost of Mordecai Richler if I could buy him a drink. He said he could use one but that he had a long drive ahead of him. Wendell Horn said the same thing. So it was that when we finally got out under the big lights of the parking lot I turned my back for just a moment and everyone else there–Wendell Horn, the ghost of Mordecai Richler, the guy on the bench who had heckled me in the weird falsetto–vanished into thin air. I wasn't surprised. I got into the car and drove back to Cleveland and had a beer in the kitchen with my wife, who wanted to know what had happened. She said I should write it down. And that is what happened, or at least, the kind of thing that *can* happen when you're talking about that old, old game, that ancient thing called baseball.

Notes on Contributors

ROBERT ALLEN, 1946-2006. A lifelong baseball enthusiast and Dodgers fan, Robert Allen was the author of over fourteen books of poetry and prose. His last book, before his untimely passing, is the epic sequence of poems *The Encantadas* (Conundrum Press).

RYAN ARNOLD is the author of *The Coward Files* (Conundrum Press). He currently lives in Vancouver.

ARJUN BASU is the editor-in-chief of *EnRoute Magazine*. He is the author of the forthcoming fiction collection, *Squishy,* from DC Books.

PAUL BEER is a writer and comedian who lives in Toronto. His work has previously appeared in *Matrix Magazine: the Awesome Issue.*

NATA BELZA is a graduate of the Creative Writing program at Concordia University and she lives and works in Montreal.

DAVE BIDINI is the co-founder of Rheostatics, author of 8 books, and the host of two award-winning documentaries, *"The Hockey Nomad"* and *"The Hockey Nomad Goes to Russia."* He lives in Toronto.

GEORGE BOWERING is the Official Loudmouth Fan of the Vancouver Canadians Baseball Club. He once threw out the first pitch before a Brewers-Reds came in Miller Stadium, Milwaukee. His latest non-fiction book is *Baseball Books* (Talonbooks), and his most recent book of poems is *Vermeer's Light* (Talonbooks). He resides in Vancouver with his score-keeper, Jean Baird.

ANDY BROWN is the publisher of Conundrum Press. Originally from Vancouver, he currently lives in Montreal. His latest book is *The Mole Chronicles* from Insomniac Press.

TAYLOR BROWN-EVANS is originally from British Columbia, and currently lives and writes in Montreal.

JASON CAMLOT is the author of *The Animal Library* and *Attention All Typewriters* (DC Books). He teaches Victorian and Romantic literature at Concordia University in Montreal. A forthcoming collection of poetry, *The Debaucher,* is due Spring '08 from Insomniac Press.

KEVIN CONNOLLY'S most recent book is *Drift* (Anansi) which was nominated for a Governor General's award. He lives and works in Toronto.

JAMES CROSBIE lives and works in Toronto.

MATT DONOVAN'S latest book is *Vellum* (Houghton-Mifflin). He currently is an assistant professor of Creative Writing at the College of Santa Fe.

STEVEN HAYWARD was born and raised in Toronto. He is an Assistant Professor at John Carroll University in Cleveland. His most recent novel, *The Secret Mitzvah of Lucio Burke* (Knopf 2005) is about a notorious baseball game that took place at Christie Pits in Toronto, in the early 1930s.

ANASTASIA JONES hails from Sudbury, Ontario. Her work has appeared in *Headlight* and *Matrix Magazine* and she was awarded Concordia University's Irving Layton Award for outstanding writing in both the poetry and prose categories. She currently is completing her doctorate in the history department at Yale University.

IAN MCGILLIS's earliest memories are a confusing mix of Canada's centennial and the Red Sox 1967 pennant run. He is the author of the novel *A Tourist's Guide to Glengarry*, in which Pirates great Roberto Clemente plays a crucial symbolic role. He cannot promise that any of his future novels will not also feature baseball in some way. He lives in Montreal. All true baseball fans will know what that means and attempt to console him.

DAVID MCGIMPSEY is the author of four collections of poetry *(Lardcake, Dogboy, Hamburger Valley, California,* and *Sitcom)* and one collection of short stories *(Certifiable)*. David has a Ph.D. in English Literature and is the author of the critically-acclaimed and award-winning study *Imagining Baseball: America's Pastime and Popular Culture.* He is a songwriter and performer–a member of the rock band Puggy Hammer and a local stand-up comedian. His travel writings frequently appear in *The Globe and Mail* and he writes the "Sandwich of the Month" column for *EnRoute* magazine. David McGimpsey currently lives in Montreal and teaches at Concordia University.

MARY MILGRAM has a Ph.D. In Creative writing from the University of Denver and is the author of many short stories and poems. She currently lives in Oman where she and her husband teach at Sultan Qaboos University. Mary grew up in Lebanon, but after spending a number of years in Massachusetts, has become a staunch Red Sox fan.

TIMOTHY MORRIS is the author of *Making the Team: the Cultural Work of Baseball Fiction* (University of Illinois Press) as well as other critical monographs. His essays have appeared in *American Scholar,* and he teaches at the University of Texas at Arlington.

ALESSANDRO PORCO is the author of *The Jill Kelly Poems*. He currently lives in Buffalo, where he is completing his doctorate at the State University of New York. A new collection, *Augustine at Carthage*, is due with ECW Books in Spring '08.

GREG SANTOS was born and raised in Montreal. His work has appeared in print and online publications, such as *McSweeney's*, the *TothWorld Podcast*, *Matrix*, *Feathertale*, and *ditch*. He lives in New Haven, CT and is in the MFA Creative Program at The New School.

DAVID TABAKOW was born in Cincinnati, Ohio. He taught English at Vanier College, has worked as a freelance writer, sold encyclopedias, and has been a counsellor at Concordia University since 1994.

Sue CHARLEBOIS

Suecharles_2000@yAhoo.coM.